ASSORTED TRIFLES

STANLEY NEWMAN

ASSORTED TRIFLES

THOUSANDS *of* TANTALIZING TRIVIA TIDBITS

RANDOM HOUSE REFERENCE

NEW YORK TORONTO LONDON SYDNEY AUKLAND

Some of the material in this book originally appeared in *10,000 Answers: The Ultimate Trivia Encyclopedia* (2001) by Stanley Newman and Hal Fittipaldi.

 Published in the United States by Random House Reference, an imprint of The Random House Information Group, a division of Random House, Inc., New York, and simultaneously in Canada by Random House of Canada Limited, Toronto.

Please address inquiries about electronic licensing of any products for use on a network, in software or on CD-ROM to the Subsidiary Rights Department, Random House Information Group, fax 212-572-6003.

This book is available for special discounts for bulk purchases for sales promotions or premiums. Special editions, including personalized covers, excerpts of existing books, and corporate imprints, can be created in large quantities for special needs. For more information, write to Random House, Inc., Special Markets/Premium Sales, 1745 Broadway, MD 6-2, New York, NY, 10019 or e-mail specialmarkets@randomhouse.com.

Visit the Random House Reference Web site: www.randomwords.com

Library of Congress Cataloging-in-Publication Data is available.

First edition

Printed in the United States of America

10 9 8 7 6 5 4 3 2 1

ISBN: 0-375-72125-8

Contents

INTRODUCTION

Welcome to *Assorted Trifles*, a compendium of wide-ranging facts in list form, designed to reward you, the random browser, with delicious tidbits wherever you look.

It is my pleasure to share with you these 200+ lists, my personal favorites of a lifetime's accumulation. Many of them first came to my attention in conjunction with my "day job" as Puzzle Editor for the New York newspaper *Newsday*. Many others are my own compilations—the result of discovering one new fact, and then digging for more like it. Some are serious, some are humorous, some are even a bit irreverent. But to make it into *Assorted Trifles*, they all had to pass the "What fun!" or "I didn't know that!" test.

Some of the material in this book originally appeared in the much larger *10,000 Answers: The Ultimate Trivia Encyclopedia* (also published by Random House), which I cowrote with Hal Fittipaldi. A few of these lists were originally compiled by Hal, who also made some very helpful suggestions about new material. Thanks, Hal.

Thanks also to my Random House editor Jena Pincott, for her skilled guidance throughout the manuscript process and for hitting upon the perfect title. I'm grateful to Jon Delfin for his meticulous proofreading of the manuscript. And thanks to the many people who graciously responded to my requests for information, most notably Dr. Steve Lomazow (America's preeminent expert on magazines' first issues), Chris Lucas of the New York City Mayor's Press Office (ticker-tape parades) and Les Waas of the Procrastinators' Club (whose quick response was an unexpected surprise).

Your comments on any aspect of this book are most welcome, as are submissions of new, original trivia tidbits. You can reach me via regular mail or e-mail at the addresses below.

If you're Internet-active, you're invited to my Web site, www.StanXwords.com. Please stop by for a visit.

STAN NEWMAN
P.O. BOX 69
MASSAPEQUA PARK, NY 11762
(Please enclose a self-addressed
stamped envelope if you'd like a reply.)

E-MAIL: StanXwords@aol.com

ASSORTED TRIFLES

CELEBRITIES *and* NOTABLE PEOPLE

Celebrities' Unusual Middle Names

Ben Affleck ....Geza

Ben Bradlee ....Crowninshield

Pearl Buck ....Sydenstricker

Dick Cavett......................Alva (same as Thomas Edison)

Dick Clark ....Wagstaff

William Faulkner ....Cuthbert

Jimmy Hoffa* ....Riddle

Elton John ....Hercules (self-selected)

Quincy Jones ....Delight

Greg Louganis................Efthimios

Nelson Mandela ....Rolihlahla (slang in the Xhosa language for "troublemaker")

Walter Matthau...............Foghorn (coined by him in 1937 for his Social Security card, still listed as such in U.S. government records)

* Last seen at a Bloomfield Hills, Michigan, restaurant on July 30, 1975

ROBERT MCNAMARA............Strange

THELONIOUS MONK.............Sphere

J.C. PENNEY ....Cash

FREDERIC REMINGTON ....Sackrider

ARNOLD SCHWARZENEGGER ..Alois

SYLVESTER STALLONE ....Enzio

UMA THURMAN ....Karuna

SPENCER TRACY.................Bonaventure

HARRY TRUMAN ....S (to honor his paternal grandfather Anderson Shippe Truman and his maternal grandfather Solomon Young)

LUTHER VANDROSS ....Ronzoni (his mother gave him this name because Ronzoni pasta was the only thing she could eat when she was pregnant with him)

• NOT UNUSUAL BUT UNEXPECTED DEPARTMENT •

Michael J. Fox's middle name is Andrew. He took the "J" as part of his stage name in honor of actor Michael J. Pollard.

People Magazine's Sexiest Man Alive

Awarded by the magazine annually since 1985 (except 1994).

1985: Mel Gibson

1986: Mark Harmon

1987: Harry Hamlin

1988: John F. Kennedy, Jr.

1989: Sean Connery

1990: Tom Cruise

1991: Patrick Swayze

1992: Nick Nolte

1993: Richard Gere and Cindy Crawford (Sexiest Couple)

1995: Brad Pitt

1996: Denzel Washington

1997: George Clooney

1998: Harrison Ford

1999: Richard Gere

2000: Brad Pitt

2001: Pierce Brosnan

2002: Ben Affleck

2003: Johnny Depp

2004: Jude Law

Time Magazine's Man/ Person of the Year

1927: Charles Lindbergh

1928: Walter P. Chrysler

1929: Owen Young (industrialist/diplomat)

1930: Mahatma Gandhi

1931: Pierre Laval

1932: Franklin D. Roosevelt

1933: Hugh Johnson (NRA Administrator)

1934: Franklin D. Roosevelt

1935: Haile Selassie

1936: Wallis Warfield Simpson

1937: General and Mme. Chiang Kai-shek

1938: Adolf Hitler

1939: Joseph Stalin

1940: Winston Churchill

1941: Franklin D. Roosevelt

1942: Joseph Stalin

1943: George C. Marshall

1944: Dwight D. Eisenhower

1945: Harry S Truman

1946: James F. Byrnes

1947: George C. Marshall

1948: Harry S Truman

1949: Winston Churchill

1950: The American Fighting Man

1951: Mohammed Mossadegh (Premier of Iran)

1952: Queen Elizabeth II

1953: Konrad Adenauer

1954: John Foster Dulles

1955: Harlow Curtice
(president of General Motors)

1956: Hungarian Freedom Fighter

1957: Nikita Khrushchev

1958: Charles de Gaulle

1959: Dwight D. Eisenhower

1960: 15 American scientists: George Beadle (geneticist); Charles Draper (engineer); John Enders (virologist); Donald Glaser (physicist); Joshua Lederberg (biologist); Willard Libby (chemist); Linus Pauling (chemist); Edward Purcell (physicist); I.I. Rabi (physicist); Emilio Segre (physicist); William Shockley (physicist); Edward Teller (physicist); Charles Townes (physicist); James Van Allen (physicist); Robert Woodward (chemist)

1961: John F. Kennedy

1962: Pope John XXIII

1963: Martin Luther King, Jr.

1964: Lyndon Johnson

1965: William Westmoreland

1966: Man and woman, 25 years old and younger

1967: Lyndon Johnson

1968: William Anders, Frank Borman, and James Lovell

1969: Middle Americans

1970: Willy Brandt

1971: Richard Nixon

1972: Richard Nixon and Henry Kissinger

1973: John Sirica

1974: King Faisal

1975: 12 American women: Susan Brownmiller (author); Kathleen Byerly (naval officer); Alison Cheek (priest); Jill Ker Conway (college president); Betty Ford; Ella Grasso (Governor of Connecticut); Carla Hills (HUD Secretary); Barbara Jordan (Texas congresswoman); Billie Jean King; Susie Sharp (North Carolina jurist); Carol Sutton (newspaper editor); Addie Wyatt (labor leader)

1976: Jimmy Carter

1977: Anwar Sadat

1978: Deng Xiaoping

1979: Ayatollah Khomeini

1980: Ronald Reagan

1981: Lech Walesa

1982: The Computer

1983: Ronald Reagan and Yuri Andropov

1984: Peter Ueberroth

1985: Deng Xiaoping

1986: Corazon Aquino

1987: Mikhail Gorbachev

1988: Endangered Earth

1989: Mikhail Gorbachev
(named Man of the Decade)

1990: George Bush

1991: Ted Turner

1992: Bill Clinton

1993: The Peacemakers: Yitzhak Rabin; Yasser Arafat; F.W. de Klerk; Nelson Mandela

1994: Pope John Paul II

1995: Newt Gingrich

1996: Dr. David Ho (AIDS researcher)

1997: Andy Grove (Intel CEO)

1998: Bill Clinton and Kenneth Starr

1999: Jeffrey Bezos (Amazon.com CEO)

2000: George W. Bush

2001: Rudolph Giuliani

2002: The whistleblowers: Cynthia Cooper (Worldcom), Sherron Watkins (Enron), Coleen Rowley (FBI)

2003: The American Soldier

2004: George W. Bush

TIME MAGAZINE'S MAN/PERSON OF THE YEAR, MULTIPLE WINNERS

THREE (1)

Franklin D. Roosevelt (1932, 1934, 1941)

TWO (12)

George W. Bush (2000, 2004)
Winston Churchill (1940, 1949)
Bill Clinton (1992, 1998)
Deng Xiaoping (1978, 1985)
Dwight D. Eisenhower (1944, 1959)
Mikhail Gorbachev (1987, 1989)
Lyndon Johnson (1964, 1967)
George C. Marshall (1943, 1947)
Richard Nixon (1971, 1972)
Ronald Reagan (1980, 1983)
Joseph Stalin (1939, 1942)
Harry S Truman (1945, 1948)

"MALE NAME" FEMALE CELEBRITIES

DREW BARRYMORE (actress, real first name Andrew)
GLENN CLOSE (actress)
JERRY HALL (model, ex-wife of Mick Jagger)
MEL HARRIS (actress, *thirtysomething*)
JOEY HEATHERTON (singer)
CECIL HOFFMANN (actress, *L.A. Law*)
JAMES KING (model/actress)

Michael Learned (actress, *The Waltons*)
Carey Lowell (actress)
Stevie Nicks (singer)
Christopher Norris (actress, *Trapper John, M.D.*)
Gene Tierney (actress)
Sean Young (actress)

Famous Brothers

Everly Brothers
Donald (born Isaac Donald, 1937)
Philip (born 1939)

Brothers Grimm
Jakob (1785-1863)
Wilhelm (1786-1859)

Brothers Karamazov
Alexei • Dmitri • Ivan

Marx Brothers
Chico (born Leonard, 1887-1961)
Harpo (born Adolph, changed to Arthur, 1888-1964)
Groucho (born Julius Henry, 1890-1977)
Gummo (born Milton, 1892-1977)
Zeppo (born Herbert, 1901-1979)

The oldest of the Marx brothers, Manfred, was born in 1885 and died in infancy.

Mayo Brothers

William (1861-1939)

Charles (1865-1939)

Righteous Brothers

Bobby Hatfield (1940-2003)

Bill Medley (born 1940)

Ringling Brothers

Albert (1852-1916)

August (1854-1907)

Otto (1858-1911)

Alfred (1861-1919)

Charles (1863-1926)

John (1866-1936)

Henry (1869-1918)

Smith Brothers

William ("Trade"*, died 1913)

Andrew ("Mark"*, died 1895)

Smothers Brothers

Dick (born 1939)

Tom (born 1937)

Warner Brothers

Harry (1881-1958)

Albert (1882-1967)

Sam (1887-1927)

Jack (1892-1978)

Dr. Joyce Brothers (born 1928)

* As erroneously assumed, based on these words appearing next to their portraits on cough-drop boxes

Famous Sisters

Andrews Sisters
Laverne (1911-1967)
Maxene (1916-1995)
Patty (born 1918)

Brontë Sisters
Anne (1820-1849)
Charlotte (1816-1855)
Elizabeth (1818-1848)

Olsen Sisters
Mary-Kate and Ashley (born 1986)*

Pointer Sisters
Anita (born 1948)
Bonnie (born 1950)
June (born 1954)
Ruth (born 1946)

Olivia de Havilland (born 1916) and **Joan Fontaine** (born Joan de Beauvoir de Havilland, 1917)

Dear Abby (born Pauline Esther Friedman, 1918) and **Ann Landers** (born Esther Pauline Friedman, 1918-2002)*

* Twin sisters

Sisters Sisters

Patricia Kalember (Georgie)
Swoosie Kurtz (Alex)
Julianne Phillips (Frankie)
Sela Ward (Teddy)

"The Seven Sisters"

NICKNAME OF THIS GROUP OF WOMEN'S COLLEGES:

Barnard College
Bryn Mawr College
Mount Holyoke College
Radcliffe College (now co-ed)
Smith College
Wellesley College
Vassar College (now co-ed)

AND THIS GROUP OF WOMEN'S SERVICE MAGAZINES:

Better Homes & Gardens
Family Circle
Good Housekeeping
Ladies' Home Journal
McCall's
Redbook
Woman's Day

Ticker-Tape Parade Honorees

Over 150 ticker-tape parades have been held in Manhattan's "Canyon of Heroes" on lower Broadway since 1886. This list omits certain honorees (such as some foreign heads of state) whose names would be unfamiliar to most people today.

October 29, 1886
Dedication of the Statue of Liberty

April 29, 1889
Centenary of the inauguration of George Washington

September 30, 1899
Return from Manila of George Dewey

June 18, 1910
Return from African safari of Theodore Roosevelt

September 8, 1919
General John J. Pershing, commander of the American Expeditionary Force

November 18, 1919
Edward, Prince of Wales (later known as the Duke of Windsor)

October 28, 1921
Ferdinand Foch, marshal of France

October 5, 1923
David Lloyd George, former English prime minister

August 6, 1924
American Olympic athletes

June 23, 1926
Flight of Richard E. Byrd and Floyd Bennett over the North Pole

July 2, 1926
Bobby Jones, winner of the British Open golf tournament

August 27, 1926
Gertrude Ederle, first woman to swim across the English Channel

June 13, 1927
Solo transatlantic flight of Charles Lindbergh

July 18, 1927
Transatlantic flight of Richard E. Byrd and the crew of the *America*

July 6, 1928
Amelia Earhart

August 22, 1928
American Olympic athletes

July 2, 1930
Bobby Jones, winner of the British Open golf tournament

July 18, 1930
Expedition to Antarctica by Richard E. Byrd

July 2, 1931
Flight around the world by Wiley Post and Harold Gatty

October 22, 1931
Pierre Laval, premier of France

June 20, 1932
Transatlantic flight of Amelia Earhart

July 26, 1933
Flight around the world in eight days by Wiley Post

July 15, 1938
Flight around the world in three days by Howard Hughes

August 5, 1938
Flight from New York City to Ireland by Douglas "Wrong Way" Corrigan

June 19, 1945
General Dwight D. Eisenhower, commander of the Allied Expeditionary Force

August 27, 1945
General Charles de Gaulle of France

September 14, 1945
General Jonathan Wainwright, hero of Corregidor

October 9, 1945
Fleet Admiral Chester Nimitz

October 27, 1945
President Harry S Truman

December 14, 1945
Fleet Admiral William S. Halsey

March 15, 1946
Former English prime minister Winston Churchill

March 19, 1948
Eamon de Valera, former prime minister of Ireland

August 19, 1949
Connie Mack, 50th year as manager of the Philadelphia Athletics baseball team

October 17, 1949
Jawaharlal Nehru, prime minister of India

April 20, 1951
General Douglas MacArthur

May 9, 1951
David Ben-Gurion, prime minister of Israel

July 7, 1952
American Olympic athletes

July 21, 1953
Ben Hogan, winner of the British Open golf tournament

June 1, 1954
Haile Selassie, emperor of Ethiopia

August 2, 1954
Syngman Rhee, president of South Korea

September 27, 1954
New York Giants, winners of the National League pennant

May 23, 1956
Sukarno, president of Indonesia

May 13, 1957
Dinh Diem, president of South Vietnam

July 11, 1957
Althea Gibson, winner of the Wimbledon women's singles championship

October 21, 1957
Queen Elizabeth II of Great Britain

May 20, 1958
Van Cliburn, winner of the Moscow International Tchaikovsky Piano Competition

February 10, 1959
Willy Brandt, mayor of West Berlin

May 29, 1959
King Baudouin of Belgium

September 11, 1959
Princess Beatrix of the Netherlands

March 9, 1960
Carol Heiss, Winter Olympics figure skating champion

April 26, 1960
Charles de Gaulle, president of France

October 19, 1960
John F. Kennedy, Democratic presidential nominee

November 2, 1960
President Dwight D. Eisenhower and Vice President Richard Nixon

April 10, 1961
New York Yankees, winners of the American League pennant

March 1, 1962
John Glenn, first American to orbit the Earth

April 9, 1962
New York Yankees, winners of the 1961 World Series

April 12, 1962
New York Mets' entry into the National League

April 16, 1962
The Shah of Iran and Empress Farah

June 5, 1962
M. Scott Carpenter, second American to orbit the Earth

June 8, 1962
Archbishop Makarios of Cyprus

May 22, 1963
L. Gordon Cooper, astronaut

October 4, 1963
Haile Selassie, emperor of Ethiopia

March 29, 1965
Virgil I. Grissom and John Young, Gemini 3 astronauts

May 19, 1965
Chung Hee Park, president of South Korea

January 10, 1969
Frank Borman, William Anders and James Lovell, Apollo 8 astronauts

August 13, 1969
Buzz Aldrin, Neil Armstrong and Michael Collins, Apollo 11 astronauts

October 20, 1969
New York Mets, winners of the World Series

October 19, 1978
New York Yankees, winners of the World Series

October 3, 1979
Pope John Paul II

January 30, 1981
The American hostages released from Iran

August 15, 1984
American Olympic medalists

May 7, 1985
Vietnam War veterans

October 28, 1986
New York Mets, winners of the World Series

June 20, 1990
Nelson Mandela of South Africa

June 10, 1991
Persian Gulf War veterans

June 25, 1991
Korean War veterans

June 17, 1994
New York Rangers, winners of the Stanley Cup

October 29, 1996
New York Yankees, winners of the World Series

October 17, 1998
Sammy Sosa, baseball player

October 23, 1998
New York Yankees, winners of the World Series

November 16, 1998
John Glenn, U.S. senator and space-shuttle astronaut

October 29, 1999
New York Yankees, winners of the World Series

October 30, 2000
New York Yankees, winners of the World Series

Ticker-Tape Parades, Multiple Honorees

Seven (1)

New York Yankees
(1961, 1962, 1978, 1996, 1998, 1999, 2000)

Three (2)

Richard E. Byrd (1926, 1927, 1930)
New York Mets (1962, 1969, 1986)

Two (7)

Charles de Gaulle (1945, 1960)
Amelia Earhart (1928, 1932)
Dwight D. Eisenhower (1945, 1960)
John Glenn (1962, 1998)
Haile Selassie (1954, 1963)
Bobby Jones (1926, 1930)
Wiley Post (1931, 1933)

Harvard University Notable Honorary Degree Recipients

1753: Benjamin Franklin

1776: George Washington

1781: John Adams

1787: Thomas Jefferson

1792: Samuel Adams

1822: John Quincy Adams

1832: Washington Irving

1833: Andrew Jackson

1859: Henry Wadsworth Longfellow

1866: Ralph Waldo Emerson

1872: Ulysses S. Grant

1896: Booker T. Washington

1905: William Howard Taft

1907: Woodrow Wilson

1917: Herbert Hoover

1919: Theodore Roosevelt

1929: Franklin D. Roosevelt

1935: Albert Einstein

1937: Robert Frost

1938: Walt Disney

1940: Carl Sandburg

1943: Winston Churchill

1946: Dwight D. Eisenhower

1951: Thornton Wilder

1956: John F. Kennedy

1961: Aaron Copland

1963: U Thant

1965: Adlai Stevenson

1966: Martha Graham

1967: Leonard Bernstein

1968: Shah of Iran

1972: Saul Bellow

1973: Georgia O'Keeffe

1973: Robert Penn Warren

1974: Ralph Ellison

1974: Beverly Sills

1976: Arthur Fiedler

1977: Eudora Welty

1978: Alexander Solzhenitsyn

1979: Desmond Tutu

1981: Ansel Adams

1981: Leontyne Price

1982: Mother Teresa

1982: Tennessee Williams

1984: King Juan Carlos I

1984: Benny Goodman

1986: Itzhak Perlman

1987: Tip O'Neill

1989: Toni Morrison

1990: Ella Fitzgerald

1990: Stephen Hawking

1990: Helmut Kohl

1991: Yo-Yo Ma

1992: Isaac Stern

1993: Colin Powell

1993: Ravi Shankar

1994: Al Gore

1995: Václav Havel

1997: Madeleine Albright

1997: Quincy Jones

1999: Alan Greenspan

2000: Seiji Ozawa

2001: Arthur Schlesinger, Jr.

2002: Daniel Patrick Moynihan

2003: Philip Roth

2004: Kofi Annan

Reuben Award

Presented annually by the National Cartoonists Society since 1946 to the Cartoonist of the Year. The statuette was designed by and named for Rube Goldberg, first president of the Society.

1946: Milton Caniff (*Terry and the Pirates*)

1947: Al Capp (*Li'l Abner*)

1948: Chic Young (*Blondie*)

1949: Alex Raymond (*Rip Kirby*)

1950: Roy Crane (*Buz Sawyer*)

1951: Walt Kelly (*Pogo*)

1952: Hank Ketcham (*Dennis the Menace*)

1953: Mort Walker (*Beetle Bailey*)

1954: Willard Mullin (Sports)

1955: Charles Schulz (*Peanuts*)

1956: Herbert L. Block a.k.a. Herblock (Editorial)

1957: Hal Foster (*Prince Valiant*)

1958: Frank King (*Gasoline Alley*)

1959: Chester Gould (*Dick Tracy*)

1960: Ronald Searle (Advertising and Illustration)

1961: Bill Mauldin (Editorial)

1962: Dik Browne (*Hi & Lois*)

1963: Fred Lasswell (*Barney Google and Snuffy Smith*)

1964: Charles Schulz (*Peanuts*)

1965: Leonard Starr (*On Stage*)

1966: Otto Soglow (*The Little King*)

1967: Rube Goldberg (Humor in Sculpture)

1968: Pat Oliphant (Editorial)

1968: Johnny Hart (*B.C.* and *The Wizard of Id*)

1969: Walter Berndt (*Smitty*)

1970: Alfred Andriola (*Kerry Drake*)

1971: Milton Caniff (*Steve Canyon*)

1972: Pat Oliphant (Editorial)

1973: Dik Browne (*Hägar the Horrible*)

1974: Dick Moores (*Gasoline Alley*)

1975: Bob Dunn (*They'll Do It Every Time*)

1976: Ernie Bushmiller (*Nancy*)

1977: Chester Gould (*Dick Tracy*)

1978: Jeff MacNelly (Editorial)

1979: Jeff MacNelly (*Shoe*)

1980: Charles Saxon (Advertising)

1981: Mell Lazarus (*Miss Peach* and *Momma)*

1982: Bil Keane (*Family Circus*)

1983: Arnold Roth (Advertising)

1984: Brant Parker (*The Wizard of Id*)

1985: Lynn Johnston (*For Better or for Worse*)

1986: Bill Watterson (*Calvin and Hobbes*)

1987: Mort Drucker (*Mad* magazine)

1988: Bill Watterson (*Calvin and Hobbes*)

1989: Jim Davis (*Garfield*)

1990: Gary Larson (*The Far Side*)

1991: Mike Peters (*Mother Goose & Grimm*)

1992: Cathy Guisewite (*Cathy*)

1993: Jim Borgman (Editorial)

1994: Gary Larson (*The Far Side*)

1995: Garry Trudeau (*Doonesbury*)

1996: Sergio Aragonés (*Mad* magazine)

1997: Scott Adams (*Dilbert*)

1998: Will Eisner (*The Spirit*)

1999: Patrick McDonnell (*Mutts*)

2000: Jack Davis (*Mad* magazine, Editorial)

2001: Jerry Scott (*Baby Blues*)

2002: Matt Groening (*The Simpsons*)

2003: Greg Evans (*Luann*)

2004: Pat Brady (*Rose is Rose*)

Prince Charles Titles

Prince Charles of Great Britain holds all of these titles:

Prince of Wales • Duke of Cornwall • Duke of Rothesay • Earl of Carrick • Lord of Renfrew • Lord of the Isles • Prince and Great Steward of Scotland • Earl of Chester

Wives of Frank Sinatra

Nancy Barbato (married 1939, divorced 1951)
Ava Gardner (married 1951, divorced 1957)
Mia Farrow (married 1966, divorced 1968)
Barbara Marx (married 1976, until Sinatra's death in 1998)

Husbands of Elizabeth Taylor

Nicky Hilton (married 1950, divorced 1951)
Michael Wilding (married 1952, divorced 1957)
Michael Todd (married 1957, widowed 1958)

Eddie Fisher (married 1959, divorced 1964)
Richard Burton (married 1964, divorced 1974)
Richard Burton (married 1975, divorced 1976)
John Warner (married 1976, divorced 1982)
Larry Fortensky (married 1991, divorced 1996)

Skull and Bones Members

Notable former members of Yale University's ultra-secret society, which has only 15 members at any one time.

George H.W. Bush
George W. Bush
W. Averell Harriman
John Kerry
Henry Luce (cofounder of Time magazine)
Archibald MacLeish (poet)
Potter Stewart (Supreme Court justice)
William Howard Taft
Robert Taft

Three Stooges' Real Names

Moe Howard ....Moses Horwitz
Larry Fine ....Louis Feinberg
Curly Howard......Jerome Lester Horwitz
Shemp Howard.....Samuel Horwitz
Joe Besser ....Jerome Besser
Joe DeRita ....Joseph Wardell

Monty Python Members

This comedy troupe was first seen on English television in the BBC series *Monty Python's Flying Circus* in 1969.

Graham Chapman • John Cleese • Terry Gilliam • Eric Idle • Terry Jones • Michael Palin

Terry Gilliam, an American, was the only non-Brit in the group.

Hello, Dolly! Title-Role Portrayers

Hello, Dolly! was the longest-running Broadway musical at the time of its closing. The portrayers of the title role during the original (1964–70) run of this Broadway play (in order):

Carol Channing • Ginger Rogers • Martha Raye • Betty Grable • Bibi Osterwald • Pearl Bailey • Phyllis Diller • Ethel Merman

Gene Autry's Cowboy Code

1. The Cowboy must never shoot first, hit a smaller man, or take unfair advantage.
2. He must never go back on his word, or a trust confided in him.
3. He must always tell the truth.

4. He must be gentle with children, the elderly, and animals.
5. He must not advocate or possess racially or religiously intolerant ideas.
6. He must help people in distress.
7. He must be a good worker.
8. He must keep himself clean in thought, speech, action, and personal habits.
9. He must respect women, parents, and his nation's laws.
10. A Cowboy is a patriot.

Procrastinator of the Year Award

Presented by the Procrastinators Club of America, not surprisingly, on an irregular basis.

1957: An ecdysiast, "For putting things off"

1964: Comedian Jack Benny, for never getting around to turning 40

1965: Murray Rappaport, for breaking the world's record for an overdue library book

1969: Dean Martin and Jerry Lewis, "Comedy Team of the Year" (more than 10 years after they split up)

1972: Elmer T. Klassen, U.S. Postmaster General, for late delivery of mail

1982: *Arizona Republic* (newspaper), for printing a September 31st edition

1988: Illinois-Central Railroad, for a train that left the station in 1903 and has yet to arrive

1991: Seafood Shanty Restaurants, for eliminating early-bird specials

1992: U.S. Congress, for tardiness in adopting a Federal budget

1995: Congressman Tom DeLay, for having such a nice name

1995: Walter Birckhead, who worked at the Melrose Diner for 50 years, starting at the age of 40

1999: "To be announced"

"The Chicago Seven"

Group of radicals tried by Judge Julius Hoffman in 1969-70 for conspiring to incite a riot at the 1968 Democratic National Convention in Chicago.

Rennie Davis • David Dellinger • John Froines • Tom Hayden • Abbie Hoffman • Jerry Rubin • Lee Weiner

The group was originally the Chicago Eight; Bobby Seale was severed from the case soon after the trial began, having been jailed for contempt for repeated verbal abuse of Judge Hoffman.

Celebrity Epitaphs

Photographs of most of these can be found at the Web site www.findagrave.com.

Mel Blanc (Warner Bros. cartoon voicemaster)
"That's all, folks"

Sonny Bono (singer/congressman)
"And the beat goes on" (He wrote and performed the song of the same name.)

F. Scott Fitzgerald (author)
"So we beat on, boats against the current, borne back ceaselessly into the past" (last line of *The Great Gatsby*)

Robert Frost (poet)
"I had a lovers quarrel with the world"

Jackie Gleason (comedian)
"And away we go" (his stage-exiting catchphrase)

Ernie Kovacs (comedian)
"Nothing in moderation"

Frederick Loewe (composer)
"Thank heaven for" (He wrote the song "Thank Heaven for Little Girls.")

Johnny Mercer (lyricist)
"And the angels sing" (He wrote the lyrics to the song of the same name.)

Satchel Paige (Hall of Fame pitcher)
The six "How to Stay Young" rules that he popularized (see page 150 for complete list)

Frank Sinatra (singer)
"The best is yet to come" (He popularized the song of the same name.)

James Van Heusen (composer)
"Swinging on a Star" (He wrote the song of the same name.)

Sir Christopher Wren (English architect)
"Si monumentum requiris, circumspice" (Latin for "If you seek his monument, look around you." At London's St. Paul's Cathedral, which he designed.)

"Unrealized" Celebrity Epitaphs

*H*umorously suggested by these celebrities, but never used.

Eddie Cantor (comedian)
"Here in nature's arms I nestle. Free at last from Georgie Jessel."

Johnny Carson (comedian/TV host)
"I'll be right back"

W.C. Fields (comedian)
"On the whole, I'd rather be in Philadelphia"

Ernest Hemingway (author)
"Pardon me for not getting up"

George S. Kaufman (playwright)
"Over my dead body"

Dorothy Parker (poet/humorist)
"Excuse my dust"

Tony Randall (actor)
"I'm not going to take this lying down"

Famous People Buried in Arlington National Cemetery

Constance Bennett (actress)
Hugo Black (Supreme Court justice)
Omar Bradley (World War II general)
William Jennings Bryan (statesman)
Richard E. Byrd (polar explorer)
Abner Doubleday (Civil War general)
William O. Douglas (Supreme Court justice)
Medgar Evers (civil-rights leader)
Virgil Grissom (astronaut)
William Halsey (World War II admiral)
Dashiell Hammett (novelist)
Oliver Wendell Holmes, Jr. (Supreme Court justice)
John F. Kennedy
Robert Kennedy
Pierre L'Enfant (designer of Washington, D.C.)
Joe Louis (boxer)
Lee Marvin (actor)
George C. Marshall (World War II general)
Thurgood Marshall (Supreme Court justice)

Audie Murphy (actor, World War II hero)
Jacqueline Kennedy Onassis
Robert Peary (polar explorer)
John J. Pershing (World War I general)
Walter Reed (bacteriologist)
Albert Sabin (polio-vaccine developer)
William Howard Taft (U.S. president, Chief Justice)
Earl Warren (Chief Justice)

Famous People Buried at Westminster Abbey

Poets/Writers

- Robert Browning
- Geoffrey Chaucer
- Charles Dickens
- John Dryden
- Thomas Hardy
- Samuel Johnson
- Rudyard Kipling
- John Masefield
- Richard Sheridan
- Edmund Spenser
- Alfred Lord Tennyson

Others

- Charles Darwin (naturalist)
- David Garrick (Shakespearean actor)

George Frideric Handel (composer)
David Livingstone (missionary/explorer)
Isaac Newton (physicist/mathematician)
Laurence Olivier (actor)
Ernest Rutherford (physicist)

Celebrity Death Date Oddities

Author Miguel de Cervantes and playwright/poet William Shakespeare both died on April 23, 1616, but Shakespeare actually died 11 days after Cervantes. Spain had already adopted the Gregorian calendar by 1616, but Great Britain remained on the Julian calendar until 1752.

Songwriter Cole Porter died on October 15, 1964, the same day that an "American Music" postage stamp was issued (honoring the 50th anniversary of the founding of ASCAP).

Actor William Demarest and pro golfer Jimmy Demaret, whose last names differ by only one letter, died on successive days (December 27th and 28th, 1983, respectively).

Actor McLean Stevenson, who portrayed Colonel Henry Blake in the TV sitcom *M*A*S*H*, and actor Roger Bowen, who had the same role in the film *MASH*, died on successive days (February 15th and 16th, 1996, respectively).

CENTENARIANS

Famous people who lived to be 100 or more.

GEORGE ABBOTT, Broadway producer (1887-1995)

IRVING BERLIN, songwriter (1888-1989)

EUBIE BLAKE, songwriter (1883-1983)

ELIZABETH BOWES-LYON, a.k.a. the Queen Mother, mother of Queen Elizabeth II (1900-2002)

GEORGE BURNS, comedian (1896-1996)

IRVING CAESAR, lyricist (1895-1996)

MADAME CHIANG KAI-SHEK (1897-2003)

JIMMIE DAVIS, Louisiana governor who wrote the tune "You Are My Sunshine" (1899-2000)

BESSIE AND SARAH DELANY, authors (1891-1995 and 1889-1999, respectively)

BOB HOPE, comedian (1903-2003)

MARY HARRIS "MOTHER" JONES, labor organizer (1830-1930)

JOSEPH NATHAN KANE, historian/reference-book author (1899-2002)

ROSE KENNEDY, presidential mother (1890-1995)

ALF LANDON, 1936 Republican presidential candidate (1887-1987)

FRANCIS LEDERER, actor (1899-2000)

JEAN MACARTHUR, wife of General Douglas MacArthur (1898-2000)

GRANDMA MOSES, painter (1860-1961)

MYRON "GRIM" NATWICK, animator who created Betty Boop (1890-1990)

IRVING RAPPER, director (1898-1999)

Leni Riefenstahl, director (1902-2003)

Hal Roach, film producer (1892-1992)

Nellie Tayloe Ross, first woman to be a state governor (1876-1977)

Sir Thomas Sopwith, aircraft designer (1888-1989)

Amos Alonzo Stagg, college football coach (1862-1965)

Strom Thurmond, senator (1902-2003)

Señor Wences, ventriloquist (1896-1999)

Estelle Winwood, actress (1882-1984)

Adolph Zukor, founder of Paramount Pictures (1873-1976)

Close, But No Cigar

Carl Barks, Disney cartoonist who created Scrooge McDuck (1901-2000)

Dave Beck, former Teamsters president (1894-1993)

Dame Barbara Cartland, romance novelist (1901-2000)

John Nance Garner, FDR's first vice president (1868-1967)

Lillian Gish, actress (October 14, 1893–February 27, 1993)

Al Hirschfeld, theater caricaturist (June 21, 1903–January 20, 2003)

Abel Kiviat, Olympic runner (1892-1991)

S.S. Kresge, retail-chain founder (1867-1966)

Georgia O'Keeffe, painter (1887-1986)

Max Schmeling, boxer (September 28, 1905–February 2, 2005)

Celebrities Born on the Same Date

• January •

January 5, 1931
choreographer Alvin Ailey, actor Robert Duvall

January 9, 1941
singer Joan Baez, actress Susannah York

January 17, 1899
mobster Al Capone, author Nevil Shute

January 21, 1941
singers Richie Havens and Plácido Domingo

January 22, 1909
actress Ann Sothern, diplomat U Thant

January 30, 1937
actress Vanessa Redgrave, chessmaster Boris Spassky

• February •

February 10, 1893
comedian Jimmy Durante, tennis pro Bill Tilden

February 10, 1898
actress Dame Judith Anderson, playwright Bertolt Brecht

February 12, 1809
naturalist Charles Darwin, U.S. president Abraham Lincoln

February 15, 1951
singer Melissa Manchester, actress Jane Seymour

February 18, 1920
game-show host Bill Cullen, actor Jack Palance

February 18, 1931
cartoonist Johnny Hart, author Toni Morrison

February 18, 1933
actress Kim Novak, Yoko Ono

February 20, 1924
actor Sidney Poitier, auto racer Bobby Unser, designer Gloria Vanderbilt

• March •

March 2, 1931
statesman Mikhail Gorbachev, author Tom Wolfe

March 21, 1962
actor Matthew Broderick, talk host Rosie O'Donnell

March 25, 1867
sculptor Gutzon Borglum, conductor Arturo Toscanini

March 31, 1935
trumpeter Herb Alpert, actor Richard Chamberlain

• April •

April 3, 1898
entertainer George Jessel, magazine publisher Henry Luce

April 3, 1924
actor Marlon Brando, actress Doris Day

April 6, 1937
singer Merle Haggard, actor Billy Dee Williams

April 7, 1939
director Francis Ford Coppola, interviewer Sir David Frost

April 20, 1893
comedian Harold Lloyd, painter Joan Miró

April 23, 1899
author Dame Ngaio Marsh, author Vladimir Nabokov

• May •

May 6, 1856
psychoanalyst Sigmund Freud, explorer Robert Peary

May 6, 1915
actor/director Orson Welles, author T.H. White

May 8, 1940
author Peter Benchley, singer Rick Nelson

May 10, 1899
dancer Fred Astaire, composer Dimitri Tiomkin

May 21, 1917
actor Raymond Burr, singer Dennis Day

May 27, 1911
statesman Hubert Humphrey, actor Vincent Price

• June •

June 1, 1926
actor Andy Griffith, actress Marilyn Monroe

June 8, 1926
artist LeRoy Neiman, comedian Jerry Stiller

June 18, 1942
reviewer Roger Ebert, singer Sir Paul McCartney

June 21, 1947
actress Meredith Baxter, actor Michael Gross (Baxter and Gross played a married couple in the TV sitcom *Family Ties*)

June 30, 1917
singer Lena Horne, drummer Buddy Rich

• July •

July 6, 1946
actor Sylvester Stallone, artist Jamie Wyeth

July 21, 1899
poet Hart Crane, author Ernest Hemingway

July 22, 1898
poet Stephen Vincent Benét, artist Alexander Calder

• October •

October 1, 1924
U.S. president Jimmy Carter, jurist William Rehnquist

• November •

November 15, 1887
poet Marianne Moore, artist Georgia O'Keeffe

• December •

December 1, 1935
actor/director Woody Allen, singer Lou Rawls

Celebrities Born and Died on the Same Date

• January •

January 16, 1935
outlaw Ma Barker (died), auto racer A.J. Foyt (born)

January 21, 1950
author George Orwell (died), singer Billy Ocean (born)

January 30, 1951
auto engineer Ferdinand Porsche (died), singer Phil Collins (born)

• February •

February 19, 1916
physicist Ernst Mach (died), jockey Eddie Arcaro (born)

• May •

May 19, 1795
biographer James Boswell (died), philanthropist Johns Hopkins (born)

May 23, 1934
outlaws Clyde Barrow and Bonnie Parker (died), inventor Robert Moog (born)

• June •

June 6, 1903
artist Paul Gauguin (died), composer Aram Khachaturian (born)

• July •

July 4, 1826
U.S. presidents John Adams and Thomas Jefferson (died), songwriter Stephen Foster (born)

July 7, 1901
author Johanna Spyri (died), director Vittorio De Sica (born)

July 22, 1932
producer Florenz Ziegfeld (died), designer Oscar de la Renta (born)

• August •

August 3, 1924
author Joseph Conrad (died), author Leon Uris (born)

• October •

October 7, 1849
author Edgar Allan Poe (died), poet James Whitcomb Riley (born)

October 15, 1917
spy Mata Hari (died), historian Arthur Schlesinger, Jr. (born)

October 26, 1902
reformer Elizabeth Cady Stanton (died), aviator Beryl Markham (born)

• November •

November 3, 1954
artist Henri Matisse (died), singer Adam Ant (born)

November 6, 1893
composer Peter Tchaikovsky (died), automaker Edsel Ford (born)

November 11, 1945
songwriter Jerome Kern (died), Nicaraguan political leader Daniel Ortega (born)

November 21, 1945
humorist Robert Benchley (died), actress Goldie Hawn (born)

November 22, 1943
lyricist Lorenz Hart (died), tennis pro Billie Jean King (born)

• December •

December 2, 1859
abolitionist John Brown (died), artist Georges Seurat (born)

December 25, 1946
comedian W.C. Fields (died), singer Jimmy Buffett (born)

FOOD *and* DRINK

International Federation of Competitive Eating Categories

This organization, which supervises and regulates eating contests, currently recognizes world records in the following categories:

asparagus • baked beans • beef tongue • bologna • buffet • burritos • butter • cabbage • candy bars • cannoli • cheesecake • chicken fingers • chicken-fried steak • chicken nuggets • chicken wings • chili • conch fritters • corn dogs • corned beef and cabbage • corned beef hash • cow brains • crawfish • doughnuts • dumplings • eggs • fruitcake • gelatin dessert • green beans • ham and potatoes • hamburgers • hamantaschen (Purim pastries) • hot dogs • hutspot (potato stew) • ice cream • jambalaya • Maine lobster • matzo balls • mayonnaise • meat pies • onions • pancakes • pasta • peas • pelemeni (Russian dumplings) • pickles • pizza • pomme frites (French fries) • pork and beans • pork ribs • posole (Mexican pork dish) • pulled pork • pumpkin pie • quesadilla • reindeer sausage • rice balls • shrimp • SPAM • Steeplechase (Ultimate Eating Tournament: shrimp, breadsticks, hot dogs, chicken wings, frozen custard) • sweet corn • sweet potato casserole • tacos • toasted ravioli • turducken (chicken stuffed in a duck stuffed in a turkey) • watermelon

More information and current records can be found at its Web site, www.ifoce.com.

LAYERS IN A MCDONALD'S BIG MAC

TOP BUN • onions • meat • pickles • lettuce • special sauce • middle bun • onions • meat • cheese • lettuce • special sauce • **BOTTOM BUN**

On average, there are 178 sesame seeds in a Big Mac bun.

BASKIN ROBBINS ORIGINAL FLAVORS

The first 31 flavors served in the first ice-cream shop opened by Burt Baskin and Irv Robbins in Glendale, California in 1948.

Banana Nut Fudge • Black Walnut • Burgundy Cherry • Butter Pecan • Butterscotch Ribbon • Chocolate • Chocolate Almond • Chocolate Chip • Chocolate Fudge • Chocolate Ribbon • Coffee • Coffee Candy • Date Nut • Egg Nog • French Vanilla • Green Mint • Lemon Crisp • Lemon Custard • Lemon Sherbet • Maple Walnut • Orange Sherbet • Peach • Peppermint Fudge • Peppermint Stick • Pineapple Sherbet • Pistachio Nut • Raspberry Sherbet • Rocky Road • Strawberry • Vanilla • Vanilla Burnt Almond

Hawaiian Punch Fruits

Juices

pineapple • orange • passionfruit • apple

Purées

apricot • papaya • guava

Jelly Belly Jelly Beans Flavors

Manufactured by the Herman Goelitz Company of Fairfield, California since 1976, they were a favorite snack of President Ronald Reagan. The 50 official flavors:

A&W Cream Soda • A&W Root Beer • Berry Blue • Blueberry • Bubble Gum • Buttered Popcorn • Café Latte • Cantaloupe • Cappuccino • Caramel Apple • Caramel Corn • Chocolate Pudding • Cinnamon • Coconut • Cotton Candy • Crushed Pineapple • Dr. Pepper • French Vanilla • Grape Jelly • Green Apple • Island Punch • Jalapeño • Juicy Pear • Kiwi • Lemon • Lemon Drop • Lemon Lime • Licorice • Mango • Margarita • Orange Juice • Orange Sherbet • Peach • Peanut Butter • Piña Colada • Pink Grapefruit • Plum • Raspberry • Red Apple • Sizzling Cinnamon • Strawberry Cheesecake • Strawberry Daiquiri • Strawberry Jam • Tangerine • Toasted Marshmallow • Top Banana • Tutti-Frutti • Very Cherry • Watermelon • Wild Blackberry

Girl Scout Cookie Best Sellers

In decreasing order of total national sales.

Thin Mints
Samoas (a.k.a. Caramel deLites)
Peanut Butter Patties (a.k.a. Tagalongs)
Peanut Butter Sandwich (a.k.a. Do-si-dos)
Shortbread (a.k.a. Trefoils)

USDA Beef Ratings

The ratings below, listed from highest to lowest, are based on two criteria: the age of the cattle (the younger the better) and the degree of marbling (intermixing of fat with lean, the more the better).

Prime • Choice • Select • Standard • Commercial • Utility • Cutter • Canner

Olive Sizes

Listed with the count ranges per pound.

Bullet (159-172)
Fine (146-159)
Brilliant (132-145)
Superior (118-132)
Large (105-118)
Extra Large (91-104)
Jumbo (83-91)
Extra Jumbo (74-82)
Giant (65-73)
Colossal (55-64)
Super Colossal (50-54)
Mammoth (46-50)
Super Mammoth (41-45)

Egg Sizes

As regulated by the USDA, listed with the minimum net weight (in ounces per dozen).

Peewee	15
Small	18
Medium	21
Large	24
Extra Large	27
Jumbo	30

Grain Weights

The standard U.S. weight (in pounds) of one bushel of each of these grains:

Barley	48
Corn (husked ears)	70
Corn (shelled)	56
Oats	32
Rye	56
Wheat	60

Sources of Herbs and Spices

Most popular herbs and spices come from plants of the same name, such as allspice, dill and ginger. These varieties are the notable exceptions:

Mace................nutmeg
Oregano..........marjoram
Paprika............chili pepper
Saffron...........crocus
Vanilla............orchid

Pasta Names

The English translation of the names of Italian pasta varieties.

Cannelloni......little tubes
Farfalle..........butterflies
Fettuccine.......little ribbons
Fusilli.............spindles
Linguine..........little tongues
Manicotti.........pipes
Mostaccioli.....little mustaches
Penne..............quills
Ravioli............little turnips
Rigatoni..........little stripes
Spaghetti.........little strings
Tortellini........little fritters
Vermicelli.......little worms

Types of Vegetarians

Listed by the degree of exclusion of animal products from the diet.

Semi-vegetarian
eats dairy products, eggs, fish and chicken

Pesco-vegetarian
eats dairy products, eggs and fish

Lacto-ovo-vegetarian (or ovo-lacto-vegetarian)
eats dairy products and eggs

Lacto-vegetarian
eats dairy products

Ovo-vegetarian
eats eggs

Vegan
eats no animal products of any kind

BUSINESS

"Generic" Name Web Sites Owned by Companies

Web sites that were presciently reserved by companies in these product categories. These companies have a "leg up" in attracting consumers who are interested in these products and services.

BLEACH.COM .... Clorox
BOOKS.COM .... Barnes & Noble
CAMERAS.COM .... E.P. Levine's (Boston camera store)
CARRENTAL.COM .... Avis/Budget
COOKIES.COM .... Adirondack Cookie Company
FLOWERS.COM 1-800-FLOWERS
FOOD.COM .... Food Network
GRAVY.COM .... Gravy Master
HOMEIMPROVEMENT.COM.. *Hometime* (PBS series)
ICECREAM.COM .... Edy's/Dreyer's
JELLY.COM .... Fischer & Weiser
LUGGAGE.COM .... Le Travel Store (San Diego store)
PAPERTOWELS.COM ...... Bounty
PEANUTBUTTER.COM ..... Skippy
PICKLES.COM .... Claussen
REALESTATE.COM .... LendingTree (mortgage broker)
RENTACAR.COM .... Avis/Budget
SALADDRESSING.COM ... Kraft
SOUP.COM .... Knorr
SPICES.COM .... Great American Spice Company
TIRES.COM .... Discount Tire Company

TOOTHPASTE.COM ....Crest
TUNA.COM ....Bumble Bee
VITAMINS.COM ....Puritan's Pride
WATER.COM ....Waters of America

Prohibited Items on eBay

Alcohol
Animals and wildlife products
Counterfeit items
Credit cards
Drugs and drug paraphernalia
Embargoed goods
Firearms and ammunition
Fireworks
Government IDs and licenses
Human body parts
Lock-picking devices
Lottery tickets
Mailing lists and personal information
Plants and seeds
Postage meters
Prescription drugs and devices
Recalled items
Satellite and cable TV descramblers
Stocks and other securities
Stolen property
Surveillance equipment
Tobacco

Business Partners

Anheuser-Busch ....Eberhard Anheuser, Adolphus Busch

Baskin Robbins ....Burton Baskin, Irvine Robbins

Bausch and Lomb ....John Jacob Bausch, Henry Lomb

Ben & Jerry's............Ben Cohen, Jerry Greenfield

Black and Decker......Samuel Black, Alonzo Decker

Currier and Ives.......Nathaniel Currier, James Ives

Dow Jones.................Charles Dow, Edward Jones

Evan-Picone ....Charles Evans, Joseph Picone

Fisher-Price ....Herman Fisher, Irving Price

Funk and Wagnalls ...Isaac Funk, Adam Wagnalls

Harley-Davidson.......William Harley; Walter, William and Arthur Davidson

H&R Block ....Henry and Richard Bloch

Hewlett Packard ....William Hewlett, David Packard

Johnson & Johnson....James Johnson, Edward Johnson

Merrill Lynch ....Charles Merrill, Edmund Lynch

PITNEY BOWES ....Arthur Pitney, Walter Bowes

PRICE WATERHOUSE ....Samuel Price, Edwin Waterhouse

RAND MCNALLY...............William Rand, Andrew McNally

ROLLS-ROYCE ....Charles Rolls, Frederick Royce

PROCTER AND GAMBLE..William Procter, James Gamble

SEARS, ROEBUCK.........Richard Sears, Alvah Roebuck

SHERWIN-WILLIAMS ....Henry Sherwin, Edward Williams

SMITH AND WESSON.....Horace Smith, Daniel Wesson

WELLS FARGO ....Henry Wells, William Fargo

DOW JONES INDUSTRIAL AVERAGE ORIGINAL STOCKS

Now consisting of 30 stocks, the Dow Jones Industrial Average was created by Charles Dow in May 1896 with these 12 stocks:

American Cotton Oil • American Sugar Refining Co. • American Tobacco • Chicago Gas • Distilling & Cattle Feeding Co. • General Electric Co. • Laclede Gas Light Co. • National Lead • North American Co. • Tennessee Coal, Iron & Railroad Co. • U.S. Leather • U.S. Rubber Co.

Dow Jones Industrial Average Milestones

November 14, 1972
First close over 1,000

January 8, 1987
First close over 2,000

April 17, 1991
First close over 3,000

February 23, 1995
First close over 4,000

November 21, 1995
First close over 5,000

October 14, 1996
First close over 6,000

February 13, 1997
First close over 7,000

July 16, 1997
First close over 8,000

April 6, 1998
First close over 9,000

March 28, 1999
First close over 10,000

Standard Oil Components

The major components of Standard Oil of New Jersey, after it was broken up by order of the U.S. Supreme Court in 1911.

Amoco ....Standard Oil of Indiana

Chevron ....Standard Oil of California

Esso (later Exxon) ...Standard Oil of New Jersey

Mobil ....Standard Oil of New York

Sohio ....Standard Oil of Ohio

One-Letter Stock-Ticker Symbols

As of this writing, the letters of the alphabet unassigned to stock-ticker symbols are H, I, J, M, P, U, V, W and Z. I and M are being reserved by the New York Stock Exchange for Intel and Microsoft, respectively, in the hope that these companies will someday trade on the NYSE.

A ....Agilent Technologies (telecommunications spin-off of Hewlett-Packard)
B ....Barnes Group (auto and airplane parts)
C ....Citigroup (formerly Citibank)
D ....Dominion Resources (Virginia power company)
E ....ENI (Italian energy company)
F ....Ford Motor Company
G ....Gillette
K ....Kellogg
L ....Liberty Financial (asset management)
N ....Inco (mining)
O ....Realty Income Corporation (real estate)
Q ....Qwest Communications (telecommunications)
R ....Ryder System (truck leasing)
S ....Sears Roebuck
T ....AT&T
X ....USX (U.S. Steel)
Y ....Alleghany Corporation (insurance, mining)

Companies' Original Names

America Online ....Quantum Computer Services

Anheuser-Busch ....Bavarian Brewery

Avon ....California Perfume Company

Bank of America........Bank of Italy

Bausch and Lomb ......Vulcanite Optical Instrument Company

Best Buy ....Sound of Music

Blockbuster Video....Cook Data Services

Boeing.......................Pacific Aero Products Company

Canon ....Seiki Kogaku Kenkyusho (Japanese for "Precision Optical Research Laboratory")

Clorox.......................Electro-Alkaline Company

CompUSA...................Soft Warehouse

Continental Airlines...Varney Speed Lines

Dell Computer ....PC's Limited

Delta Air Lines ....Huff-Daland Dusters

Green Giant ....Minnesota Valley Canning Company

H&R Block ....United Business Company

IBM ....Computing-Tabulating-Recording Company

J.C. PENNEY................Golden Rule Stores

L'ORÉAL......................French Harmless Hair Dye Company

MET LIFE.....................National Union Life and Limb Insurance Company

NIKE...........................Blue Ribbon Sports

PRUDENTIAL INSURANCE..Widows and Orphans Friendly Society

QUAKER OATS..............American Cereal Company

RALSTON-PURINA.........Robinson-Danforth Commission Company

SNAPPLE.....................Unadulterated Food Products

SONY..........................Tokyo Tsushin Denki (Japanese for "Tokyo Telecommunications Engineering")

TEXAS INSTRUMENTS....Geophysical Service Inc.

TOYS "R" US..............Children's Supermart

UNITED PARCEL SERVICE..American Messenger Company

UNITED WAY................Community Chests and Councils of America

U.S. AIRWAYS..............All-American Aviation

WHIRLPOOL.................Upton Machine Company

XEROX........................Haloid Company

"4 C's"

The four standards by which diamonds are judged by the Gemological Institute of America.

Carats

The larger the diamond, the more valuable, and the more valuable per carat.

Clarity, or lack of inclusions (minute traces of noncrystallized carbon)

Fl (flawless)
IF (internally flawless)
VVS1-VVS2 (very very slightly included)
VS1-VS2 (very slightly included)
SI1-SI3 (slightly included)
I1-I3 (included)

Color (the closer to colorless, the more valuable), on a scale of D to Z

D-F (colorless)
G-J (near colorless)
K-M (faint yellow)
N-R (very light yellow)
S-Z (light yellow)
Z+ is used to indicate a fancy color

Cut

How well the diamond has been cut to produce the maximum return of light. (This is different from the shape of the diamond, which is not in itself a determinant of value.)

Movies

Unlikely Singers in Films

Warren Beatty and Dustin Hoffman
"That's Amore" and "Strangers in the Night" in *Ishtar*

Candice Bergen
"Better Than Ever" in *Starting Over*

Ingrid Bergman
"The Children's Marching Song" in *The Inn of the Sixth Happiness*

Irving Berlin
"Oh, How I Hate to Get Up in the Morning" in *This Is the Army*

Shirley Booth
"I'm in the Mood for Love" in *About Mrs. Leslie*

Ernest Borgnine
"The Best Things in Life Are Free" in *The Best Things in Life Are Free*

Marlon Brando
"Luck Be a Lady" and "I'll Know" in *Guys and Dolls*

Mel Brooks and Anne Bancroft
"Sweet Georgia Brown" (sung in Polish) in *To Be or Not to Be*

Yul Brynner

"Mad About the Boy" in *The Magic Christian*

Sean Connery

"Pretty Irish Girl" in *Darby O'Gill and the Little People*

Billy Crystal and Meg Ryan

"Surrey With the Fringe on Top" in *When Harry Met Sally…*

Bette Davis

"I've Written a Letter to Daddy" in *Whatever Happened to Baby Jane?*

Robert De Niro

"Blue Moon" in *New York, New York*

Kirk Douglas

"Pretty Little Girl in the Yellow Dress" in *The Last Sunset*

Charles Durning

"Mary's a Grand Old Name" in *Tootsie*

Clint Eastwood

"I Talk to the Trees" and "Gold Fever" in *Paint Your Wagon*

Henry Fonda
"Red River Valley" in *The Grapes of Wrath*

Clark Gable
"Puttin' on the Ritz" in *Idiot's Delight*

Jackie Gleason
"Call Me Irresponsible" in *Papa's Delicate Condition*

Oliver Hardy
"Honolulu Baby" in *Sons of the Desert*

Audrey Hepburn
"La Vie en Rose" in *Sabrina*

Diane Keaton
"Seems Like Old Times" in *Annie Hall*

Sophia Loren
"Bing! Bang! Bong!" in *Houseboat*

Lee Marvin
"The First Thing You Know" and "Wand'rin' Star" in *Paint Your Wagon*

Peter O'Toole
"The Impossible Dream" in *Man of La Mancha*

Jason Robards
"Bye Bye Blackbird" in *Melvin and Howard*

Will Rogers

"When the Blue of the Night Meets the Gold of the Day" in *Doubting Thomas*

Sylvester Stallone

"Too Close to Paradise" in *Paradise Alley*

Spencer Tracy

"Don't Cry Little Fish" in *Captains Courageous*

Gene Wilder and Peter Boyle

"Puttin' on the Ritz" in *Young Frankenstein*

James Bond Film Songs/Singers

Where no song title is below, the title is the same as the film's title. The first Bond film, *Dr. No* (1962), had no title song.

***From Russia With Love* (1963):** Matt Monro

***Goldfinger* (1964):** Shirley Bassey

***Thunderball* (1965):** Tom Jones

***You Only Live Twice* (1967):** Nancy Sinatra

***Casino Royale* (1967):** Herb Alpert and the Tijuana Brass

***On Her Majesty's Secret Service* (1969):** "We Have All the Time in the World"—Louis Armstrong

***Diamonds Are Forever* (1971):** Shirley Bassey

Live and Let Die (1973): Paul McCartney and Wings

The Man With the Golden Gun (1974): Lulu

The Spy Who Loved Me (1977): "Nobody Does It Better"—Carly Simon

Moonraker (1979): Shirley Bassey

For Your Eyes Only (1981): Sheena Easton

Octopussy (1983): "All Time High"—Rita Coolidge

Never Say Never Again (1983): Lani Hall

A View to a Kill (1985): Duran Duran

The Living Daylights (1987): a-ha

Licence to Kill (1989): Gladys Knight

GoldenEye (1995): Tina Turner

Tomorrow Never Dies (1997): Sheryl Crow

The World Is Not Enough (1999): Garbage

Die Another Day (2002): Madonna

*Shirley Bassey (*Goldfinger, Diamonds Are Forever *and* Moonraker*) is the only artist to perform the opening song in more than one James Bond film.*

SINGERS IN JOHN WAYNE FILMS

These performers (with one or more *Billboard* U.S. top-40 tunes to their credit) are listed below with the John Wayne film(s) in which they appeared.

PAUL ANKA.................*The Longest Day*

ANN-MARGRET............*The Train Robbers*

FRANKIE AVALON.........*The Alamo*

PAT BOONE ....*The Greatest Story Ever Told*

WALTER BRENNAN........*Red River, Rio Bravo* and five others

RED BUTTONS ....*Hatari, The Longest Day*

GLEN CAMPBELL ....*True Grit*

JOHNNY CRAWFORD......*El Dorado*

BING CROSBY.............*Cancel My Reservation**

FABIAN......................*North to Alaska*

PHIL HARRIS ....*The High and the Mighty*

TAB HUNTER ....*The Sea Chase*

DEAN MARTIN.............*Rio Bravo, The Sons of Katie Elder*

* WAYNE AND CROSBY MAKE CAMEO APPEARANCES IN THIS FILM

Sal Mineo.................*The Longest Day, The Greatest Story Ever Told*

Ricky Nelson............*Rio Bravo*

Fess Parker..............*Island in the Sky*

Debbie Reynolds.......*How the West Was Won*

Tommy Sands.............*The Longest Day*

Frank Sinatra...........*Cast a Giant Shadow*

Bobby Vinton............*Big Jake, The Train Robbers*

Fred Astaire/ Ginger Rogers Films

Flying Down to Rio (1933)
The Gay Divorcee (1934)
Roberta (1935)
Top Hat (1935)
Swing Time (1936)
Follow the Fleet (1936)
Shall We Dance (1937)
Carefree (1938)
The Story of Vernon and Irene Castle (1939)
The Barkleys of Broadway (1949)

Judy Garland/ Mickey Rooney Films

Thoroughbreds Don't Cry (1937)
Love Finds Andy Hardy (1938)
Babes in Arms (1939)
Strike Up the Band (1940)
Andy Hardy Meets Debutante (1940)
Babes on Broadway (1941)
Life Begins for Andy Hardy (1941)
Girl Crazy (1943)
Thousands Cheer (1943)
Words and Music (1948)

"Road" Films

Series starring Bing Crosby, Bob Hope and Dorothy Lamour.

Road to Singapore (1940)
Road to Zanzibar (1941)
Road to Morocco (1942)
Road to Utopia (1945)
Road to Rio (1947)
Road to Bali (1952)
The Road to Hong Kong (1962)

Katharine Hepburn/ Spencer Tracy Films

Keeper of the Flame (1942)
Woman of the Year (1942)
Without Love (1945)
The Sea of Grass (1947)
State of the Union (1948)
Adam's Rib (1949)
Pat and Mike (1952)
Desk Set (1957)
Guess Who's Coming to Dinner (1967)

Elizabeth Taylor/ Richard Burton Films

Cleopatra (1963)
The V.I.P.s (1963)
The Sandpiper (1965)
Who's Afraid of Virginia Woolf? (1966)
The Taming of the Shrew (1967)
Doctor Faustus (1967)
The Comedians (1967)
Boom! (1968)
Anne of the Thousand Days (1969)*
Hammersmith Is Out (1972)
Under Milk Wood (1973)

* Taylor has a cameo role in this film

GROUCHO MARX ROLES

HAMMER..................... *The Cocoanuts* (1929)

CAPTAIN JEFFREY
T. SPAULDING.............. *Animal Crackers* (1930)

GROUCHO .... *Monkey Business* (1931)

PROFESSOR QUINCY
ADAMS WAGSTAFF .... *Horse Feathers* (1932)

RUFUS T. FIREFLY .... *Duck Soup* (1933)

OTIS B. DRIFTWOOD ..... *A Night at the Opera* (1935)

DR. HUGO Z. HACKENBUSH . *A Day at the Races* (1937)

J. CHEEVER LOOPHOLE.. *At the Circus* (1939)

S. QUENTIN QUALE....... *Go West* (1940)

WOLF J. FLYWHEEL....... *The Big Store* (1941)

RONALD KORNBLOW ..... *A Night in Casablanca* (1946)

LIONEL Q. DEVERAUX ... *Copacabana* (1947)

SAM GRUNION .... *Love Happy* (1949)

EMILE J. KECK............. *Double Dynamite* (1951)

GEORGE SCHMIDLAP..... *Will Success Spoil Rock Hunter?* (1957)*

PETER MINUIT .... *The Story of Mankind* (1957)

GOD........................... *Skidoo* (1968)

* CAMEO ROLE

A Night at the Opera "Stateroom" Scene

The 15 people crowded into the tiny cabin in the famous scene of the 1935 Marx Brothers film.

Otis B. Driftwood (Groucho) • Fiorello (Chico) • Tomasso (Harpo) • Ricardo Baroni (Allan Jones) • two maids • an engineer • a manicurist • the engineer's assistant • a girl looking for her Aunt Minnie • a washwoman • four stewards

Seven Dwarfs

As seen in the 1937 Disney animated film *Snow White and the Seven Dwarfs*.

Bashful

Doc: the leader, and the only one wearing glasses

Dopey: the only one without a beard, the only one with blue eyes, and the only one who never speaks

Grumpy

Happy: the only one without thin, dark eyebrows; his are white and bushy

Sleepy

Sneezy

They are all brothers, and are all diamond miners.

Fantasia Sections

The musical selections heard in the original 1940 Disney film.

Toccata and Fugue in D minor
Johann Sebastian Bach

Nutcracker Suite ("Dance of the Sugarplum Fairy," "Chinese Dance," "Dance of the Flutes," "Russian Dance," "Waltz of the Flowers")
Peter Tchaikovsky

"The Sorcerer's Apprentice"
Paul Dukas

The Rite of Spring
Igor Stravinsky

Symphony #6 (Pastoral Symphony)
Ludwig van Beethoven

"Dance of the Hours"
Amilcare Ponchielli

"A Night on Bald Mountain"
Modest Mussorgsky

"Ave Maria"
Franz Schubert

Fantasia/2000 Sections

Every section after the first has a celebrity introduction.

Symphony #5 (First Movement)
Ludwig van Beethoven

The Pines of Rome
Ottorino Respighi
(Steve Martin, Itzhak Perlman)

Rhapsody in Blue
George Gershwin (Quincy Jones)

Piano Concerto #2 (Allegro)
Dmitri Shostakovich (Bette Midler)

Carnival of the Animals
Camille Saint-Saëns (James Earl Jones)

"The Sorcerer's Apprentice"
Paul Dukas (Penn and Teller)

"Pomp and Circumstance"
Sir Edward Elgar (James Levine, conductor of the orchestra)

Firebird Suite
Igor Stravinsky (Angela Lansbury)

"Who's on First?" Team

In the order mentioned in the 1945 Abbott and Costello film *The Naughty Nineties.*

Who ....first base
What ....second base
I Don't Know ......third base
Why.....................left field
Because ....center field
Tomorrow ....pitcher
Today ....catcher
I Don't Care ....shortstop

No right fielder is mentioned in the routine.

The Dirty Dozen Title Characters

Tassos Bravos (Al Mancini)
Victor Franko (John Cassavetes)
Glenn Gilpin (Ben Carruthers)
Robert Jefferson (Jim Brown)
Pedro Jiminez (Trini Lopez)
Roscoe Lever (Stuart Cooper)
Archer Maggott (Telly Savalas)
Vernon Pinkley (Donald Sutherland)
Samson Posey (Clint Walker)
Seth Sawyer (Colin Maitland)
Milo Vladek (Tom Busby)
Joseph Wladislaw (Charles Bronson)

The Magnificent Seven Title Characters

Bernardo O'Reilly (Charles Bronson)
Britt (James Coburn)
Chico (Horst Buchholz)
Chris Adams (Yul Brynner)
Harry Luck (Brad Dexter)
Lee (Robert Vaughn)
Vin (Steve McQueen)

Bronson is the only actor to portray one of the title characters in both The Dirty Dozen *and* The Magnificent Seven.

Close Encounters

As publicized for the 1977 Steven Spielberg film *Close Encounters of the Third Kind.*

CLOSE ENCOUNTER OF THE FIRST KIND
sighting of a UFO

CLOSE ENCOUNTER OF THE SECOND KIND
physical evidence

CLOSE ENCOUNTER OF THE THIRD KIND
contact

The Lion King Voices and Roles

Rowan Atkinson (Zazu, hornbill)
Matthew Broderick (Simba, title character)
Whoopi Goldberg (Shenzi, hyena)
Robert Guillaume (Rafiki, mandrill)
Jeremy Irons (Scar, uncle of Simba)
James Earl Jones (Mufasa, father of Simba)
Moira Kelly (Nala, girlfriend of Simba)
Nathan Lane (Timon, meerkat)
Cheech Marin (Banzai, hyena)
Ernie Sabella (Pumbaa, warthog)
Madge Sinclair (Sarabi, mother of Simba)
Jonathan Taylor Thomas (young Simba)

Batman Forever Riddles

The riddles posed by The Riddler (Jim Carrey) to Batman and Robin (Val Kilmer and Chris O'Donnell, respectively) in the 1995 film. They were written by Will Shortz, crossword editor of the *New York Times*.

If you look at the numbers upon my
face, you won't find 13 anyplace.

Tear off one and scratch my head.
What once was red is black instead.

The eight of us go forth, not back,
to protect a king from a foe's attack.

We're five little items of an everyday sort.
You'll find us all in a tennis court.

Answers: A clock, a match, chess pawns, and the five vowels (a, e, i, o, u)

Multiple Academy Award-Winning Actors

Four-time winners (1)

Katharine Hepburn: *Morning Glory* (1933), *Guess Who's Coming to Dinner* (1967), *The Lion in Winter* (1968), *On Golden Pond* (1981)

Three-time winners (3)

Ingrid Bergman: *Gaslight* (1944), *Anastasia* (1956), *Murder on the Orient Express* (1974*)

Walter Brennan: *Come and Get It* (1936*), *Kentucky* (1938*), *The Westerner* (1940*)

Jack Nicholson: *One Flew Over the Cuckoo's Nest* (1975), *Terms of Endearment* (1983*), *As Good as It Gets* (1997)

* Award was for a supporting role

Two-time winners (31)

Marlon Brando: *On the Waterfront* (1954), *The Godfather* (1972)

Michael Caine: *Hannah and Her Sisters* (1986*), *The Cider House Rules* (1999*)

Bette Davis: *Dangerous* (1935), *Jezebel* (1938)

Olivia de Havilland: *To Each His Own* (1946), *The Heiress* (1949)

Robert De Niro: *The Godfather Part II* (1974*), *Raging Bull* (1980)

Melvyn Douglas: *Hud* (1963*), *Being There* (1979*)

Sally Field: *Norma Rae* (1979), *Places in the Heart* (1984)

Jane Fonda: *Klute* (1971), *Coming Home* (1978)

Jodie Foster: *Accused* (1988), *The Silence of the Lambs* (1991)

Gene Hackman: *The French Connection* (1971), *Unforgiven* (1992*)

Tom Hanks: *Philadelphia* (1993), *Forrest Gump* (1994)

Helen Hayes: *The Sin of Madelon Claudet* (1931), *Airport* (1970*)

Dustin Hoffman: *Kramer vs. Kramer* (1979), *Rain Man* (1988)

Glenda Jackson: *Women in Love* (1970), *A Touch of Class* (1973)

Jessica Lange: *Tootsie* (1982*), *Blue Sky* (1994)

Vivien Leigh: *Gone With the Wind* (1939), *A Streetcar Named Desire* (1951)

Jack Lemmon: *Mister Roberts* (1955*), *Save the Tiger* (1973)

Fredric March: *Dr. Jekyll and Mr. Hyde* (1932), *The Best Years of Our Lives* (1946)

Anthony Quinn: *Viva Zapata!* (1952*), *Lust for Life* (1956*)

Luise Rainer: *The Great Ziegfeld* (1936), *The Good Earth* (1937)

Jason Robards: *All the President's Men* (1976*), *Julia* (1977*)

Maggie Smith: *The Prime of Miss Jean Brodie* (1969), *California Suite* (1978*)

Kevin Spacey: *The Usual Suspects* (1995*), *American Beauty* (1999)

Meryl Streep: *Kramer vs. Kramer* (1979*), *Sophie's Choice* (1982)

* Award was for a supporting role

Hilary Swank: *Boys Don't Cry* (1999), *Million Dollar Baby* (2004)

Elizabeth Taylor: *Butterfield 8* (1960), *Who's Afraid of Virginia Woolf?* (1966)

Spencer Tracy: *Captains Courageous* (1937), *Boys Town* (1938)

Peter Ustinov: *Spartacus* (1960*), *Topkapi* (1964*)

Denzel Washington: *Glory* (1989*), *Training Day* (2001)

Dianne Wiest: *Hannah and Her Sisters* (1986*), *Bullets Over Broadway* (1994*)

Shelley Winters: *The Diary of Anne Frank* (1959*), *A Patch of Blue* (1965*)

Knighted Movie Actors

Richard Attenborough
Alan Bates
Dirk Bogarde
Michael Caine
Charlie Chaplin
Sean Connery
John Gielgud
Alec Guinness
Cedric Hardwicke
Rex Harrison
Nigel Hawthorne
Ian Holm
Anthony Hopkins
Derek Jacobi
Ben Kingsley
Ian McKellen
John Mills
Roger Moore
Laurence Olivier
Anthony Quayle
Michael Redgrave
Ralph Richardson
Peter Ustinov

"Dame" Movie Actresses

Dames of the British Empire are the female equivalent of knights.

Judith Anderson
Julie Andrews
Peggy Ashcroft
Gladys Cooper
Judi Dench
Edith Evans
Wendy Hiller
Celia Johnson
Helen Mirren
Diana Rigg
Flora Robson
Margaret Rutherford
Maggie Smith
Elizabeth Taylor
Sybil Thorndike
May Whitty

Multiple Academy Award-Winning Directors

Four-Time Winners (1)

John Ford: *The Informer* (1935), *The Grapes of Wrath* (1940), *How Green Was My Valley* (1941), *The Quiet Man* (1952)

Three-Time Winners (2)

Frank Capra: *It Happened One Night* (1934), *Mr. Deeds Goes to Town* (1936), *You Can't Take It With You* (1938)

William Wyler: *Mrs. Miniver* (1942), *The Best Years of Our Lives* (1946), *Ben-Hur* (1959)

Two-Time Winners (15)

Frank Borzage: *7th Heaven* (1927), *Bad Girl* (1931)

Clint Eastwood: *Unforgiven* (1992), *Million Dollar Baby* (2004)

Milos Forman: *One Flew Over the Cuckoo's Nest* (1975), *Amadeus* (1984)

Elia Kazan: *Gentleman's Agreement* (1947), *On the Waterfront* (1954)

David Lean: *The Bridge on the River Kwai* (1957), *Lawrence of Arabia* (1962)

Frank Lloyd: *The Divine Lady* (1929), *Cavalcade* (1933)

Joseph L. Mankiewicz: *A Letter to Three Wives* (1949), *All About Eve* (1950)

Leo McCarey: *The Awful Truth* (1937), *Going My Way* (1944)

Lewis Milestone: *Two Arabian Knights* (1927), *All Quiet on the Western Front* (1930)

Steven Spielberg: *Schindler's List* (1993), *Saving Private Ryan* (1998)

George Stevens: *A Place in the Sun* (1951), *Giant* (1956)

Oliver Stone: *Platoon* (1986), *Born on the Fourth of July* (1989)

Billy Wilder: *The Lost Weekend* (1945), *The Apartment* (1960)

Robert Wise: *West Side Story* (1961), *The Sound of Music* (1965)

Fred Zinnemann: *From Here to Eternity* (1953), *A Man for All Seasons* (1966)

Directors' First Feature Films

Woody Allen .... *Take the Money and Run* (1969)

Robert Altman .... *The Delinquents* (1957)

Peter Bogdanovich ... *Targets* (1968)

Mel Brooks .... *The Producers* (1968)

Tim Burton .... *Pee-wee's Big Adventure* (1985)

James Cameron .... *Piranha Part Two: The Spawning* (1981)

Frank Capra .... *The Strong Man* (1926)

Joel Coen .... *Blood Simple* (1984)

Francis Ford Coppola .. *Dementia 13* (1963)

Wes Craven .... *Last House on the Left* (1972)

George Cukor .... *Grumpy* (1930)

Cecil B. DeMille........*The Squaw Man* (1914)

Jonathan Demme ....*Caged Heat* (1974)

Clint Eastwood ....*Play Misty for Me* (1974)

John Frankenheimer .*The Young Stranger* (1957)

Alfred Hitchcock ......*The Pleasure Garden* (1925)

John Huston ....*The Maltese Falcon* (1941)

Elia Kazan.................*A Tree Grows in Brooklyn* (1945)

Stanley Kramer ....*Not as a Stranger* (1955)

Stanley Kubrick........*Fear and Desire* (1953)

John Landis...............*Schlock* (1971)

David Lean ....*In Which We Serve* (1942)

Spike Lee...................*She's Gotta Have It* (1986)

Barry Levinson.........*Diner* (1982)

David Lynch...............*Eraserhead* (1978)

Joseph L. Mankiewicz *Dragonwyck* (1946)

Vincente Minnelli .....*Cabin in the Sky* (1943)

Mike Nichols............*Who's Afraid of Virginia Woolf?* (1966)

Roman Polanski ....*Knife in the Water* (1962)

Sydney Pollack ....*The Slender Thread* (1965)

MARTIN SCORSESE .... *Who's That Knocking at My Door* (1968)

RIDLEY SCOTT .... *The Duellists* (1977)

STEVEN SODERBERGH... *sex, lies and videotape* (1989)

STEVEN SPIELBERG ...... *The Sugarland Express* (1974)

OLIVER STONE............. *Seizure* (1974)

QUENTIN TARANTINO .... *Reservoir Dogs* (1992)

ORSON WELLES .... *Citizen Kane* (1941)

WIM WENDERS .... *Hammett* (1983)*

BILLY WILDER .... *The Major and the Minor* (1942)*

ROBERT WISE.............. *The Curse of the Cat People* (1944)

WILLIAM WYLER .... *Crook Buster* (1925)

ROBERT ZEMECKIS .... *I Wanna Hold Your Hand* (1978)

DIRECTORS' LAST FEATURE FILMS

FRANK CAPRA .... *Pocketful of Miracles* (1961)

GEORGE CUKOR .... *Rich and Famous* (1981)

CECIL B. DEMILLE........ *The Ten Commandments* (1956)

ALFRED HITCHCOCK ...... *Family Plot* (1976)

JOHN HUSTON .... *The Dead* (1987)

* FIRST ENGLISH-LANGUAGE FILM

Elia Kazan................. *The Last Tycoon* (1976)

Stanley Kramer .... *The Runner Stumbles* (1979)

Stanley Kubrick........ *Eyes Wide Shut* (1999)

David Lean .... *A Passage to India* (1984)

Joseph L. Mankiewicz.. *Sleuth* (1972)

Vincente Minnelli ..... *A Matter of Time* (1976)

Orson Welles .... *F for Fake* (1974)

Billy Wilder .... *Buddy Buddy* (1981)

Robert Wise.............. *Rooftops* (1989)

William Wyler .... *The Liberation of L.B. Jones* (1970)

National Film Awards

The awards comparable to the Academy Award in other countries.

Australia
Lovely

Canada
Genie

France
César

Great Britain
BAFTA

Italy
David di Donatello

Sweden
Guldbagge (golden ram)

Spain
Goya

Mexico
Ariel

Taiwan
Golden Horse

Film Ratings

The Motion Picture Association of America introduced voluntary ratings for films on November 1, 1968, superseding the Hays Production Code previously in effect.

• Original 1968 Ratings •

G ...General Audiences (all ages admitted)

M...Mature Audiences (all ages admitted, but parental guidance suggested)

R...Restricted (children under 16 not admitted without a parent or guardian, later raised to 17)

X...no one under 17 admitted

• Name Changes/Additions •

1969: M changed to GP

1970: GP changed to PG

1984: PG split into PG and PG-13 ("Parents strongly cautioned. Some material may be inappropriate for pre-teenagers")

1990: X changed to NC-17

"The Hollywood Ten"

Group of nine screenwriters and one director, blacklisted for refusing to testify before the House Un-American Activities Committee in 1947.

Alvah Bessie • Herbert Biberman • Lester Cole • Edward Dmytryk (director) • Ring Lardner, Jr. • John Howard Lawson • Albert Maltz • Samuel Ornitz • Adrian Scott • Dalton Trumbo

Composer Biopics

Classical Music

Ludwig van Beethoven (Gary Oldman)
Immortal Beloved (1994)

Frédéric Chopin (Cornel Wilde)
A Song to Remember (1945)

Edvard Grieg (Toralv Maurstad)
Song of Norway (1970)

George Frideric Handel (Wilfrid Lawson)
The Great Mr. Handel (1942)

Franz Liszt (Dirk Bogarde)
Song Without End (1960)

Franz Liszt (Roger Daltrey)
Lisztomania (1975)

Gustav Mahler (Robert Powell)
Mahler (1974)

Wolfgang Amadeus Mozart (Tom Hulce)
Amadeus (1984)

Rimsky-Korsakov (Jean-Pierre Aumont)
Song of Scheherazade (1947)

Franz Schubert (Alan Curtis)
New Wine (1941)

Johann Strauss, Jr. (Fernand Gravet)
The Great Waltz (1938)

Johann Strauss, Jr. (Horst Buchholz)
The Great Waltz (1972)

Peter Tchaikovsky (Richard Chamberlain)
The Music Lovers (1971)

Richard Wagner (Alan Badel)
Magic Fire (1956)

Richard Wagner (Richard Burton)
Wagner (1983)

Popular Music

Ernest R. Ball (Dick Haymes)
Irish Eyes Are Smiling (1944)

George M. Cohan (James Cagney)
Yankee Doodle Dandy (1942)

Daniel Decatur Emmett (Bing Crosby)
Dixie (1943)

Paul Dresser (Victor Mature)
My Gal Sal (1942)

Stephen Foster (Douglass Montgomery)
Harmony Lane (1935)

Stephen Foster (Don Ameche)
Swanee River (1939)

Stephen Foster (Bill Shirley)
I Dream of Jeannie (1952)

George Gershwin (Robert Alda)
Rhapsody in Blue (1945)

Gilbert and Sullivan (Robert Morley and Maurice Evans, respectively)
The Great Gilbert and Sullivan (1953)

Gilbert and Sullivan (Jim Broadbent and Allan Corduner, respectively)
Topsy-Turvy (1999)

Woody Guthrie (David Carradine)
Bound for Glory (1976)

W.C. Handy (Nat "King" Cole)
St. Louis Blues (1958)

Victor Herbert (Walter Connolly)
The Great Victor Herbert (1939)

Joseph E. Howard (Mark Stevens)
I Wonder Who's Kissing Her Now (1947)

Scott Joplin (Billy Dee Williams)
Scott Joplin (1977)

Gus Kahn (Danny Thomas)
I'll See You in My Dreams (1951)

Bert Kalmar and Harry Ruby (Fred Astaire and Red Skelton, respectively)
Three Little Words (1950)

Jerome Kern (Robert Walker)
Till the Clouds Roll By (1946)

Cole Porter (Cary Grant)
Night and Day (1946)

Cole Porter (Kevin Kline)
De-Lovely (2004)

Rodgers and Hart (Tom Drake and Mickey Rooney, respectively)
Words and Music (1946)

Sigmund Romberg (Jose Ferrer)
Deep in My Heart (1954)

John Philip Sousa (Clifton Webb)
Stars and Stripes Forever (1952)

Fictional Presidents in Films

With character name, if any.

Mason Adams
The Final Conflict (1981)

Eddie Albert
Dreamscape (1984)

Alan Alda
Canadian Bacon (1995)

Dan Aykroyd (William Haney)
My Fellow Americans (1996)

Jim Backus
Slapstick (of Another Kind) (1984)

Ed Begley
The Monitors (1969)

Richard Belzer
Species II (1998)

POLLY BERGEN (LESLIE MCCLOUD)
Kisses for My President (1964)

JEFF BRIDGES (JACKSON EVANS)
The Contender (2000)

LLOYD BRIDGES (THOMAS "TUG" BENSON)
Hot Shots! Part Deux (1993)

RONNY COX (JACK NEIL)
Murder at 1600 (1997)

JAMES CROMWELL (ROBERT FOWLER)
The Sum of All Fears (2002)

ROBERT CULP
The Pelican Brief (1993)

MICHAEL DOUGLAS (ANDREW SHEPHERD)
The American President (1995)

ANDREW DUGGAN (PRESIDENT TRENT)
In Like Flint (1967)

CHARLES DURNING (DAVID STEVENS)
Twilight's Last Gleaming (1977)

HENRY FONDA
Fail-Safe (1964)

HENRY FONDA
Meteor (1979)

HARRISON FORD (JAMES MARSHALL)
Air Force One (1997)

James Franciscus (James Cassidy)
The Greek Tycoon (1978)

Morgan Freeman (Tom Beck)
Deep Impact (1998)

James Garner (Matt Douglas)
My Fellow Americans (1996)

George Gobel
Rabbit Test (1978)

Gene Hackman (Allen Richmond)
Absolute Power (1997)

Gene Hackman (Monroe Eagle Cole)
Welcome to Mooseport (2004)

Mark Harmon (James Foster)
Chasing Liberty (2004)

Hal Holbrook (Adam Scott)
The Kidnapping of the President (1980)

Michael Keaton (President Mackenzie)
First Daughter (2004)

Kevin Kline (Bill Mitchell)
Dave (1993)

Harvey Korman
Jingle All the Way (1996)

Jack Lemmon (Russell P. Kramer)
My Fellow Americans (1996)

Fredric March (Jordan Lyman)
Seven Days in May (1964)

E.G. Marshall
Superman II (1980)

Bob Newhart (Manfred Link)
First Family (1980)

Jack Nicholson (James Dale)
Mars Attacks! (1996)

Gregory Peck
Amazing Grace and Chuck (1987)

Donald Pleasence
Escape From New York (1981)

Bill Pullman (Thomas J. Whitmore)
Independence Day (1996)

John Ritter (Chet Roosevelt)
Americathon (1979)

Tim Robbins
Austin Powers: The Spy Who Shagged Me (1999)

Cliff Robertson
Escape From L.A. (1996)

Roy Scheider (President Carlson)
Executive Target (1997)

Roy Scheider (Robert Baker)
The Peacekeeper (1997)

Roy Scheider (Jack Cahill)
Chain of Command (2000)

Franchot Tone
Advise & Consent (1962)

Jack Warden ("Bobby")
Being There (1979)

William Windom
Escape From the Planet of the Apes (1971)

Screen Actors Guild Presidents

1933: Ralph Morgan

1933-35: Eddie Cantor

1935-38: Robert Montgomery

1939-40: Ralph Morgan

1940-42: Edward Arnold

1942-44: James Cagney

1944-46: George Murphy

1946-47: Robert Montgomery

1947-52: Ronald Reagan

1952-57: Walter Pidgeon

1957-58: Leon Ames

1958-59: Howard Keel

1959-60: Ronald Reagan

1960-63: George Chandler

1963-65: Dana Andrews

1965-71: Charlton Heston

1971-73: John Gavin

1973-75: Dennis Weaver

1975-79: Kathleen Nolan

1979-81: William Schallert

1981-85: Edward Asner

1985-88: Patty Duke

1988-95: Harry Gordon

1995-99: Richard Masur

1999-2001: William Daniels

2001—PRESENT: Melissa Gilbert

Television

Mickey Mouse Club Famous Alumni

Original Series (1955-59)

Don Agrati (a.k.a. Don Grady of *My Three Sons*)
Johnny Crawford (*The Rifleman*)
Annette Funicello
Paul Petersen (*The Donna Reed Show*)

Revival (1989-95)

Christina Aguilera
J.C. Chasez ('NSYNC)
Ryan Gosling (*Young Hercules*)
Keri Russell (*Felicity*)
Britney Spears
Justin Timberlake ('NSYNC)

Mickey Mouse Club Theme Days

As seen on the original 1955-59 series.

Monday ....Fun With Music Day

Tuesday ....Guest Star Day

Wednesday................Anything Can Happen Day

Thursday ....Circus Day

Friday........................Talent Round-Up Day

CHARLIE'S ANGELS TITLE CHARACTERS

From the 1976-81 TV series.

1976-79: Sabrina Duncan (Kate Jackson)

1976-77: Jill Munroe (Farrah Fawcett-Majors)
Kelly Garrett (Jaclyn Smith)

1977-81: Kris Munroe (Cheryl Ladd)

1979-80: Tiffany Welles (Shelley Hack)

1980-81: Julie Rogers (Tanya Roberts)

BATMAN VILLAINS

There was a guest-star "villain of the week" on each episode of this 1966-68 series.

THE ARCHER (Art Carney)
THE BLACK WIDOW (Tallulah Bankhead)
THE BOOKWORM (Roddy McDowall)
DR. CASSANDRA (Ida Lupino)
CATWOMAN (Julie Newmar, Eartha Kitt)
CHANDELL (Liberace)
NORA CLAVICLE (Barbara Rush)
CLOCK KING (Walter Slezak)
EGGHEAD (Vincent Price)
FALSEFACE (Malachi Throne)
MR. FREEZE (George Sanders, Otto Preminger, Eli Wallach)
COLONEL GUMM (Roger C. Carmel)

The Joker (Cesar Romero)
Louie the Lilac (Milton Berle)
The Mad Hatter (David Wayne)
Marsha, Queen of Diamonds (Carolyn Jones)
Minerva (Zsa Zsa Gabor)
The Minstrel (Van Johnson)
Olga, Queen of the Cossacks (Anne Baxter)
Ma Parker (Shelley Winters)
The Penguin (Burgess Meredith)
Lord Phogg (Rudy Vallee)
The Puzzler (Maurice Evans)
The Riddler (Frank Gorshin, John Astin)
The Sandman (Michael Rennie)
Shame (Cliff Robertson)
The Siren (Joan Collins)
King Tut (Victor Buono)
Zelda the Great (Anne Baxter)

Lee Meriwether portrayed Catwoman in the 1966 feature film based on the TV series, but did not play the role on the series itself.

Game Shows Hosted by Bill Cullen

Cullen hosted 20 TV game shows, more than anyone else.

Winner Take All (1952)
Give and Take (1952)
Bank on the Stars (1953–54)
Place the Face (1954–55)
Name That Tune (1954–55)
Down You Go (1956)

The Price Is Right (1956-65)
Eye Guess (1966-69)
Three on a Match (1971-74)
The $25,000 Pyramid (1974-79)
Winning Streak (1974-75)
Blankety Blanks (1975)
I've Got a Secret (1976)
Pass the Buck (1978)
The Love Experts (1978-79)
Chain Reaction (1980)
Blockbusters (1980-1982)
Child's Play (1982-83)
Hot Potato (1984)
The Joker's Wild (1984-1986)

Cullen also appeared as a substitute host on Break the Bank *(1950s) and* Password Plus *(1980).*

1959-60 Westerns

This season was the peak of the Westerns craze, with a record 26 Westerns on the prime-time TV schedule for the full 1959-60 season:

Bat Masterson
Black Saddle
Bonanza
Bronco
Cheyenne
Colt .45
The Deputy
Dick Powell's Zane Grey Theater
Gunsmoke
Have Gun Will Travel
Johnny Ringo
Laramie
The Lawman
Law of the Plainsman
The Life and Legend of Wyatt Earp
The Man From Blackhawk
Maverick
Rawhide
The Rebel
The Rifleman
Sugarfoot
Tales of Wells Fargo
The Texan
Wagon Train
Wanted: Dead or Alive
Wichita Town

Real-Life Sitcom Settings

As opposed to fictional locales.

Alice..........................Phoenix, Arizona

All in the Family ......New York City (Queens)

Amos 'n' Andy ....New York City (Manhattan)

Barney Miller ....New York City (Manhattan)

The Beverly Hillbillies.................Beverly Hills, California

Bewitched ....Westport, Connecticut

The Bob Newhart Show..........................Chicago, Illinois

Caroline in the City ....New York City (Manhattan)

Cheers ....Boston, Massachusetts

Chico and the Man ...East Los Angeles, California

The Cosby Show........New York City (Brooklyn)

Designing Women ......Atlanta, Georgia

Dharma & Greg ....San Francisco, California

The Dick Van Dyke Show.........................New Rochelle, New York

Diff'rent Strokes.....New York City (Manhattan)

THE DREW CAREY SHOW..........................Cleveland, Ohio

EMPTY NEST...............Miami, Florida

EVERYBODY LOVES RAYMOND...................Lynbrook, New York

FAMILY TIES...............Columbus, Ohio

FRASIER......................Seattle, Washington

FRIENDS......................New York City (Manhattan)

FULL HOUSE................San Francisco, California

THE GOLDBERGS..........New York City (Bronx)

THE GOLDEN GIRLS......Miami, Florida

GOOD TIMES...............Chicago, Illinois

GROWING PAINS..........Huntington, New York

HAPPY DAYS...............Milwaukee, Wisconsin

HEAD OF THE CLASS....New York City (Manhattan)

HOME IMPROVEMENT....Detroit, Michigan

THE HONEYMOONERS...New York City (Brooklyn)

I DREAM OF JEANNIE...Cocoa Beach, Florida

I LOVE LUCY...............New York City (Manhattan)

THE JEFFERSONS.........New York City (Manhattan)

Just Shoot Me ....New York City (Manhattan)

Kate & Allie ....New York City (Manhattan)

Laverne & Shirley ....Milwaukee, Wisconsin; Burbank, California

Mad About You.........New York City (Manhattan)

Malcolm & Eddie ......Kansas City, Missouri

Mama ....San Francisco, California

Martin ....Detroit, Michigan

The Mary Tyler Moore Show..............Minneapolis, Minnesota

M*A*S*H....................Uijongbu, South Korea

Maude........................Tuckahoe, New York

Mork & Mindy...........Boulder, Colorado

Mr. Belvedere..........Beaver Falls, Pennsylvania

Murphy Brown..........Washington, D.C.

My Favorite Martian.....................Los Angeles, California

My Little Margie......New York City (Manhattan)

The Nanny................New York City (Manhattan)

Night Court.............New York City (Manhattan)

The Odd Couple ....New York City (Manhattan)

One Day at a Time ....Indianapolis, Indiana

The Patty Duke Show ....New York City (Brooklyn)

Perfect Strangers ...Chicago, Illinois

Rhoda ....New York City (Manhattan)

Sanford and Son ......Los Angeles, California

Seinfeld....................New York City (Manhattan)

Spin City ....New York City (Manhattan)

Taxi ....New York City (Manhattan)

That Girl ....New York City (Manhattan)

That's My Mama ....Washington, D.C.

Three's Company ......Santa Monica, California

Too Close for Comfort ....San Francisco, California

Welcome Back Kotter ....New York City (Brooklyn)

Who's the Boss?.......Fairfield, Connecticut

Will & Grace ....New York City (Manhattan)

Wings ....Nantucket, Massachusetts

Music

Top Five Singles on U.S. *Billboard* Pop Chart for the Week of April 4, 1964

This was the only time that the same person/group held all the top five positions on this chart.

#1: "Can't Buy Me Love" (Beatles)
#2: "Twist and Shout" (Beatles)
#3: "She Loves You" (Beatles)
#4: "I Want to Hold Your Hand" (Beatles)
#5: "Please Please Me" (Beatles)

Beatles #1 Tunes

These 20 tunes all reached #1 on the U.S. Billboard pop chart:

"I Want to Hold Your Hand" (1964)
"She Loves You" (1964)
"Can't Buy Me Love" (1964)
"Love Me Do" (1964)
"A Hard Day's Night" (1964)
"I Feel Fine" (1964)
"Eight Days a Week" (1965)
"Ticket to Ride" (1965)
"Help!" (1965)
"Yesterday" (1965)
"We Can Work It Out" (1965)
"Paperback Writer" (1966)
"Penny Lane" (1967)

"All You Need Is Love" (1967)
"Hello Goodbye" (1967)
"Hey Jude" (1968)
"Get Back" (1969)
"Come Together" (1969)
"Let It Be" (1970)
"The Long and Winding Road" (1970)

Elvis Presley #1 Tunes

These 18 tunes all reached #1 on the U.S. Billboard pop chart:

"Heartbreak Hotel" (1956)
"I Want You, I Need You, I Love You" (1956)
"Hound Dog" (1956)
"Don't Be Cruel" (1956)
"Love Me Tender" (1956)
"Too Much" (1957)
"All Shook Up" (1957)
"(Let Me Be Your) Teddy Bear" (1957)
"Jailhouse Rock" (1957)
"Don't" (1958)
"Hard Headed Woman" (1958)
"A Big Hunk o' Love" (1959)
"Stuck on You" (1960)
"It's Now or Never" (1960)

"Are You Lonesome Tonight?" (1960)
"Surrender" (1961)
"Good Luck Charm" (1962)
"Suspicious Minds" (1969)

James Brown Nicknames

"The Godfather of Soul"
"The Hardest Working Man in Show Business"
"Mr. Dynamite"
"Mr. Please Please"
"Soul Brother Number One"

Rock and Roll Hall of Fame Charter Members

The first-year performer inductees of 1986.

Chuck Berry
James Brown
Ray Charles
Sam Cooke
Fats Domino
Everly Brothers
Buddy Holly
Jerry Lee Lewis
Elvis Presley
Little Richard

Woodstock '69 Performers

The acts that appeared on the main stage of the Woodstock Music and Arts Fair, at Bethel, New York on August 15-17, 1969.

August 15

Richie Havens
Country Joe McDonald
John Sebastian
Incredible String Band
Bert Sommer
Sweetwater
Tim Hardin
Ravi Shankar
Melanie
Arlo Guthrie
Joan Baez

August 16

Quill
Keef Hartley
Santana
Mountain
Canned Heat
Grateful Dead
Creedence Clearwater Revival
Janis Joplin
Sly and the Family Stone
The Who
Jefferson Airplane

August 17

Joe Cocker
Country Joe and the Fish
Ten Years After
The Band
Blood, Sweat and Tears
Johnny Winter
Crosby, Stills, Nash and Young
Paul Butterfield Blues Band
Sha Na Na
Jimi Hendrix

"WET"

1984 Barbra Streisand "theme" album, where the title of each song pertains to the theme. Album cuts included:

"Wet"
"Come Rain or Come Shine"
"Splish Splash"
"On Rainy Afternoons"
"After the Rain"
"No More Tears"
"Niagara"
"I Ain't Gonna Cry Tonight"
"Kiss Me in the Rain"

MAJOR RECORDING ARTISTS WHO NEVER WON A GRAMMY AWARD

Roy Acuff • The Beach Boys • Chuck Berry • Patsy Cline • Sam Cooke • Creedence Clearwater Revival • Bing Crosby • Fats Domino • The Doors • The Drifters • The Four Tops • Benny Goodman • Grateful Dead • Lionel Hampton • Jimi Hendrix • Jackson Five • Jefferson Airplane • Led Zeppelin • Bob Marley • "Little Richard" Penniman • Diana Ross • Rod Stewart • Supremes • Three Dog Night • Lawrence Welk • Kitty Wells • The Who

Elvis Presley never won a Grammy Award in the pop-music category. His three Grammys were all for Gospel recordings.

Selected Works of P.D.Q. Bach

"The last and by far the least child of the great Johann Sebastian Bach." The discovery/creation of Peter Schickele.

1712 Overture

The Art of the Ground Round

Breakfast Antiphonies

Canine Cantata

Christmas Carols: "Throw the Yule Log on, Uncle John," "O Little Town of Hackensack," "Good King Kong Looked Out"

Concerto for Horn and Hardart

Concerto for Two Pianos vs. Orchestra

Echo Sonata for Two Unfriendly Groups of Instruments

Fanfare for Fred

Fanfare for the Common Cold

Four Curmudgeonly Canons

Four Folk Song Upsettings

Fuga Meshuga

"Goldbrick" Variations

Grand Serenade for an Awful Lot of Winds and Percussion

Hansel & Gretel & Ted & Alice

"Howdy" Symphony

Iphigenia in Brooklyn

Lip My Reeds

March of the Cute Little Wood Sprites

Missa Hilarious

My Bonnie Lass She Smelleth
No-No Nonette
Octoot
Oedipus Tex
The Only Piece Ever Written for Violin and Tuba
Overture to *La Clemenza di Genghis Khan*
Overture to *The Abduction of Figaro*
The Preachers of Crimetheus, Ballet in One Selfless Act
Prelude to *Einstein on the Fritz*
The Queen to Me a Royal Pain Doth Give
Royal Firewater Musick
"Safe" Sextet
Schleptet
The Seasonings
Shepherd on the Rocks, With a Twist
The Short-Tempered Clavier
Three Teeny Preludes
"Unbegun" Symphony
Variations on an Unusually Simple-Minded Theme

BEETHOVEN SONATA NICKNAMES

"Pathétique"..................#8
"Moonlight"..................#14
"Pastoral".......................#15
"Waldstein"....................#21
"Appassionata" ....#23
"Hammerklavier"..........#29

Peter and the Wolf Characters/Instruments

This symphonic fairy tale for narrator and orchestra was written by Russian composer Sergei Prokofiev in 1936, to teach the instruments of the orchestra to children. The characters below are represented by the indicated instruments in the piece.

Bird ....flute
Duck..oboe
Cat ....clarinet
Grandfather ....bassoon
Wolf ....French horns
Peter ....strings
Rifle shots of the hunters......kettledrum and bass drum

Grand Piano Sizes

5'8" ....Baby grand
5'10" ....Living Room grand
6'...............................Professional grand
6'4" ....Drawing Room grand
6'8" ....Parlour grand
7'4" ....Half Concert grand
8'11" or longer ....Concert grand

Symphony Nicknames

"1905" ....Shostakovich's #11
"1917" ....Shostakovich's #12
"Afternoon"..............................Haydn's #7
"The Age of Anxiety" ....Bernstein's #2
"Alleluia" ....Haydn's #30
"Antarctica" ....Vaughan Williams' #7
"Apocalyptic"............................Bruckner's #7
"Babi-Yar" ....Shostakovich's #13
"Bear" ....Haydn's #82
"Chase".......................................Haydn's #73
"Choral" ....Beethoven's #9
"Classical" ....Prokofiev's #1
"Clock" ....Haydn's #101
"Dance"......................................Copland's #1
"Dante" ....Liszt (unnumbered)
"Drum Roll"...............................Haydn's #103
"Eroica"......................................Beethoven's #3
"Evening"..................................Haydn's #8
"Farewell"................................Haydn's #45
"Faust" ....Liszt (unnumbered)
"Fire"..Haydn's #59
"First of May"..........................Shostakovich's #3
"Great, The" ....Schubert's #9
"Haffner"...................................Mozart's #35

"HEN" ....Haydn's #83
"HORN SIGNAL" ....Haydn's #31
"IMPERIAL" ....Haydn's #53
"ITALIAN" ....Mendelssohn's #4
"JEREMIAH" ....Bernstein's #1
"JUPITER" ....Mozart's #41
"LAMENTATION" ....Haydn's #26
"LAUDON" ....Haydn's #69
"LENINGRAD" ....Shostakovich's #7
"LINZ" ....Mozart's #36
"LITTLE RUSSIAN" ....Tchaikovsky's #2
"LONDON" ....Vaughan Williams' #2
"LONDON SYMPHONIES" ....Haydn's #93-104
"MARIA THERESA" ....Haydn's #48
"MERCURY" ....Haydn's #43
"MILITARY" ....Haydn's #100
"MIRACLE" ....Haydn's #96
"MORNING" ....Haydn's #6
"(FROM THE) NEW WORLD" ....Dvorák's #9
"NORDIC" ....Hanson's #1
"OCTOBER" ....Shostakovich's #2
"OXFORD" ....Haydn's #92
"PARIS" ....Mozart's #31
"PARIS SYMPHONIES" ....Haydn's #82-87
"PASSION" ....Haydn's #49
"PASTORAL" ....Beethoven's #6, Milhaud's #2, Vaughan Williams' #3

"Pathétique" ....Tchaikovsky's #6
"Philosopher" ....Haydn's #22
"Polish" ....Tchaikovsky's #3
"Prague" ....Mozart's #38
"Queen" ....Haydn's #85
"Reformation" ....Mendelssohn's #5
"Requiem" ....Hanson's #4
"Resurrection" ....Mahler's #2
"Rhenish" ....Schumann's #3
"Romantic" ....Bruckner's #4,
Hanson's #2
"Schoolmaster" ....Haydn's #55
"Scottish" ....Mendelssohn's #3
"Sea" ....Hanson's #7,
Vaughan Williams'
#1
"Serenade" ....Milhaud's #3
"Short" ....Copland's #2
"Spring" ....Milhaud's #1,
Schumann's #1
"Surprise" ....Haydn's #94
"Thousand, Symphony of a" ......Mahler's #8
"Toy" ....Haydn
(unnumbered)
"Tragic" ....Haydn's #44,
Schubert's #4
"Unfinished" ....Schubert's #8
"Wagner" ....Bruckner's #3
"Winter Daydreams" ....Tchaikovsky's #1

Girl Crazy Opening-Night Orchestra

The October 14, 1930, Broadway opening of this George and Ira Gershwin musical included this remarkable assemblage of jazz greats:

Jimmy Dorsey
Benny Goodman
Gene Krupa
Glenn Miller
Red Nichols (leader)
Jack Teagarden

Rodgers and Hammerstein Musicals

Oklahoma! (1943, Broadway)
State Fair (1945, film)
Carousel (1945, Broadway)
Allegro (1947, Broadway)
South Pacific (1949, Broadway)
The King and I (1951, Broadway)
Me and Juliet (1953, Broadway)
Pipe Dream (1955, Broadway)
Cinderella (1957, television)
Flower Drum Song (1958, Broadway)
The Sound of Music (1959, Broadway)

LITERATURE *and the* PRINTED WORD

"Fellowship of the Ring" Members

The original nine members from the first book of J.R.R. Tolkien's *Lord of the Rings* trilogy.

Aragorn, a.k.a. Strider (human)
Boromir (human)
Frodo Baggins (hobbit)
Gandalf (wizard)
Gimli (dwarf)
Legolas (elf)
Meriadoc "Merry" Brandybuck (hobbit)
Peregrin "Pippin" Took (hobbit)
Samwise "Sam" Gamgee (hobbit)

"Alphabet" Mysteries

Ongoing series of whodunits written by Sue Grafton.

"A" Is for Alibi (1982)
"B" Is for Burglar (1985)
"C" Is for Corpse (1986)
"D" Is for Deadbeat (1987)
"E" Is for Evidence (1988)
"F" Is for Fugitive (1989)
"G" Is for Gumshoe (1990)
"H" Is for Homicide (1991)
"I" Is for Innocent (1992)
"J" Is for Judgment (1993)
"K" Is for Killer (1994)
"L" Is for Lawless (1995)
"M" Is for Malice (1996)
"N" Is for Noose (1998)
"O" Is for Outlaw (1999)
"P" Is for Peril (2001)
"Q" Is for Quarry (2002)
"R" Is for Ricochet (2004)
"S" Is for Silence (2005)

Canterbury Tales Tales

The Knight's Tale
The Miller's Tale
The Reeve's Tale
The Cook's Tale
The Man of Law's Tale
The Wife of Bath's Tale
The Friar's Tale
The Summoner's Tale
The Clerk's Tale
The Merchant's Tale
The Squire's Tale
The Franklin's Tale
The Physician's Tale
The Pardoner's Tale
The Shipman's Tale
The Prioress' Tale
The Tale of Sir Thopas
The Tale of Melibee
The Monk's Tale
The Nun's Priest's Tale
The Second Nun's Tale
The Canon's Yeoman's Tale
The Manciple's Tale
The Parson's Tale

"Rabbit" Tetralogy

Series of four books by John Updike with Harry "Rabbit" Angstrom as the main character.

Rabbit, Run (1960)
Rabbit Redux (1971)
Rabbit Is Rich (1981)
Rabbit at Rest (1990)

The last two books were each awarded a Pulitzer Prize. Updike's 2000 book Licks of Love *includes the novella "Rabbit Remembered," a postscript to the series.*

REMEMBRANCE OF THINGS PAST

Novel in seven parts by French author Marcel Proust.

Swann's Way (1913)
Within a Budding Grove (1919)
The Guermantes Way (1920)
Cities of the Plain (1921)
The Captive (1923)
The Sweet Cheat Gone (1925)
Time Regained (1927)

HOGWARTS REQUIRED READING

From the Harry Potter series of books by English author J.K. Rowling.

FIRST YEAR

The Standard Book of Spells, Grade 1 by Miranda Goshawk
A History of Magic by Bathilda Bagshot
Magical Theory by Adalbert Waffling
A Beginner's Guide to Transfiguration by Emeric Switch
One Thousand Magical Herbs and Fungi by Phyllida Spore
Magical Drafts and Potions by Arsenius Jigger
Fantastic Beasts and Where to Find Them by Newt Scamander
The Dark Forces: A Guide to Self-Protection by Quentin Trimble

Second Year

The Standard Book of Spells, Grade 2 by Miranda Goshawk
Break With a Banshee by Gilderoy Lockhart
Gadding With Ghouls by Gilderoy Lockhart
Holidays With Hags by Gilderoy Lockhart
Travels With Trolls by Gilderoy Lockhart
Voyages With Vampires by Gilderoy Lockhart
Wanderings With Werewolves by Gilderoy Lockhart
Year With the Yeti by Gilderoy Lockhart

Third Year

The Standard Book of Spells, Grade 3 by Miranda Goshawk
Intermediate Transfiguration by Emeric Switch
The Monster Book of Monsters
Unfogging the Future by Cassandra Vablatsky
Numerology and Gramatica
Ancient Runes Made Easy
Home Life and Social Habits of Muggles
various rune dictionaries

Fourth Year

The Standard Book of Spells, Grade 4 by Miranda Goshawk
Numerology and Gramatica

Fifth Year

The Standard Book of Spells, Grade 5 by Miranda Goshawk
The Dream Oracle
Defensive Magical Theory by Wilbert Slinkhard

The Chronicles of Narnia

Series of seven children's books by C.S. Lewis.

The Lion, the Witch and the Wardrobe (1950)
Prince Caspian (1951)
The Voyage of the "Dawn Treader" (1952)
The Silver Chair (1953)
The Horse and His Boy (1954)
The Magician's Nephew (1955)
The Last Battle (1956)

Shakespeare Opening Lines

Opening lines from selected plays of William Shakespeare, listed below with the speaker of the line.

Antony and Cleopatra

"Nay, but this dotage of our general's
O'erflows the measure" (Philo)

The Comedy of Errors

"Proceed, Solinus, to procure my fall
And by the doom of death end woes and all"
(Aegeon)

Hamlet

"Who's there?" (Bernardo)

Julius Caesar

"Home! home, you idle creatures, get you home!"
(Flavius)

King Henry IV, Part II

"Open your ears; for which of you will stop
The vent of hearing when loud Rumour
speaks?" (Rumour, the Presenter)

King Henry V

"O for a Muse of fire, that would ascend
The brightest heaven of invention,
A kingdom for a stage, princes to act
And monarchs to behold the swelling scene!"
(Chorus)

King Henry VI, Part I

"Hung be the heavens with black, yield day to
night!" (Duke of Bedford)

King Henry VIII

"I come no more to make you laugh: things now
That bear a weighty and a serious brow,
Sad, high, and working, full of state and woe,
Such noble scenes as draw the eye to flow,
We now present." (From the Prologue)

King Lear

"I thought the King had more affected the Duke
of Albany than Cornwall." (Earl of Kent)

Macbeth

"When shall we three meet again
In thunder, lightning, or in rain?" (First Witch)

The Merry Wives of Windsor

"Sir Hugh, persuade me not; I will make a Star-
chamber matter of it; if he were twenty Sir John

Falstaffs, he shall not abuse Robert Shallow, esquire." (JUSTICE SHALLOW)

A Midsummer Night's Dream

"Now, fair Hippolyta, our nuptial hour
Draws on apace; four happy days bring in
Another moon" (THESEUS, DUKE OF ATHENS)

Othello

"Tush! never tell me; I take it much unkindly
That thou, Iago, who hast had my purse
As if the strings were thine, shouldst know of this." (RODERIGO)

Pericles, Prince of Tyre

"To sing a song that old was sung,
From ashes ancient Gower is come;
Assuming man's infirmities,
To glad your ear, and please your eyes."
(GOWER)

Richard III

"Now is the winter of our discontent
Made glorious summer by this sun of York;
And all the clouds that lour'd upon our house
In the deep bosom of the ocean buried."
(RICHARD, DUKE OF GLOUCESTER)

Romeo and Juliet

"Two households, both alike in dignity,
In fair Verona, where we lay our scene,

From ancient grudge break to new mutiny,
Where civil blood makes civil hands unclean."
(CHORUS)

THE TAMING OF THE SHREW

"I'll pheeze you, in faith." (CHRISTOPHER SLY)

THE TEMPEST

"Boatswain!" (SHIP-MASTER)

TITUS ANDRONICUS

"Noble patricians, patrons of my right,
Defend the justice of my cause with arms,
And, countrymen, my loving followers,
Plead my successive title with your swords"
(SATURNINUS)

TROILUS AND CRESSIDA

"In Troy, there lies the scene."
(FROM THE PROLOGUE)

TWELFTH NIGHT

"If music be the food of love, play on"
(ORSINO, DUKE OF ILLYRIA)

THE WINTER'S TALE

"If you shall chance, Camillo, to visit Bohemia, on the like occasion whereon my services are now on foot, you shall see, as I have said, great difference betwixt our Bohemia and your Sicilia." (ARCHIDAMUS)

Expressions From *Don Quixote de la Mancha*

All of these common expressions originated from the Miguel de Cervantes book.

A finger in every pie
Born with a silver spoon in one's mouth
Forewarned is forearmed
Give the devil his due
Honesty is the best policy
Mum's the word
No love lost
The pot calling the kettle black
The proof of the pudding is in the eating
Raise a hue and cry
The sky's the limit
A stone's throw
Smell a rat
Thank you for nothing
Time out of mind
Turn over a new leaf
Too much of a good thing
Wild-goose chase
A word to the wise is sufficient

Authors' First Novels

Louisa May Alcott.....*The Inheritance* (1849)

L. Frank Baum...........*Father Goose* (1899)

Saul Bellow.............*Dangling Man* (1944)

Pearl S. Buck...........*East Wind, West Wind* (1930)

Edgar Rice Burroughs...............*Tarzan of the Apes* (1914)

Albert Camus............*The Stranger* (1942)

Truman Capote..........*Other Voices, Other Rooms* (1948)

Barbara Cartland.....*Jigsaw* (1925)

Willa Cather.............*Alexander's Bridge* (1912)

Raymond Chandler....*The Big Sleep* (1939)

John Cheever............*The Wapshot Chronicle* (1957)

Agatha Christie........*The Mysterious Affair at Styles* (1920)

Tom Clancy...............*The Hunt for Red October* (1984)

Mary Higgins Clark...*Where Are the Children?* (1975)

James Fenimore Cooper.*Precaution* (1820)

Len Deighton............*The Ipcress File* (1962)

Philip K. Dick............*Solar Lottery* (1955)

Charles Dickens.......*The Pickwick Papers* (1836-37)

E.L. Doctorow...........*Welcome to Hard Times* (1960)

John Dos Passos.......*One Man's Initiation: 1917* (1920)

Theodore Dreiser.....*Sister Carrie* (1900)

William Faulkner......*Soldier's Pay* (1926)

Edna Ferber............*Dawn O'Hara* (1911)

F. Scott Fitzgerald...*This Side of Paradise* (1920)

E.M. Forster............*Where Angels Fear to Tread* (1905)

ZANE GREY .... *Betty Zane* (1904)

JOHN GRISHAM .... *A Time to Kill* (1988)

DASHIELL HAMMETT ..... *Red Harvest* (1929)

NATHANIEL HAWTHORNE .... *Fanshawe* (1828)

ROBERT A. HEINLEIN .... *Rocket Ship Galileo* (1947)

ERNEST HEMINGWAY .... *The Sun Also Rises* (1926)

JOHN HERSEY .... *A Bell for Adano* (1944)

ALDOUS HUXLEY .... *Crome Yellow* (1921)

JOHN IRVING .... *Setting Free the Bears* (1969)

HENRY JAMES .... *Watch and Ward* (1871)

JAMES JOYCE .... *A Portrait of the Artist as a Young Man* (1916)

FAYE KELLERMAN .... *Ritual Bath* (1986)

JACK KEROUAC .... *The Town and the City* (1950)

STEPHEN KING .... *Carrie* (1974)

IRA LEVIN .... *A Kiss Before Dying* (1953)

SINCLAIR LEWIS .... *Hike and the Aeroplane* (1912)

JACK LONDON .... *The Son of the Wolf* (1900)

NORMAN MAILER .... *The Naked and the Dead* (1948)

BERNARD MALAMUD ..... *The Natural* (1952)

Thomas Mann .... *Buddenbrooks* (1901)

Somerset Maugham ... *Lisa of Lambeth* (1897)

Carson McCullers .... *The Heart Is a Lonely Hunter* (1940)

Larry McMurtry .... *Horseman, Pass By* (1961)

Herman Melville .... *Typee* (1846)

Flannery O'Connor ... *Wise Blood* (1952)

John O'Hara .... *Appointment in Samarra* (1934)

Thomas Pynchon .... V (1963)

Anne Rice .... *Interview With the Vampire* (1976)

Philip Roth .... *Letting Go* (1962)

Sidney Sheldon .... *The Naked Face* (1970)

John Steinbeck .... *Cup of Gold* (1929)

William Styron .... *Lie Down in Darkness* (1951)

Booth Tarkington ..... *The Gentleman From Indiana* (1899)

Mark Twain .... *The Gilded Age* (1873)

John Updike .... *The Poorhouse Fair* (1959)

Gore Vidal .... *Williwaw* (1946)

Kurt Vonnegut .... *Player Piano* (1960)

Robert Penn Warren .. *Night Rider* (1939)

Evelyn Waugh ....*Decline and Fall* (1928)

Edith Wharton..........*The Valley of Decision* (1902)

Thornton Wilder......*Cabala* (1926)

Profiles in Courage Subjects

John F. Kennedy's Pulitzer Prize-winning 1956 book profiles these eight Americans who took politically risky positions:

John Quincy Adams
Thomas Hart Benton
Sam Houston
Lucius Quintus Cincinnatus Lamar
George Norris
Edmund G. Ross
Robert Taft
Daniel Webster

The Second World War

The six volumes of the epic work by Winston Churchill.

The Gathering Storm (1948)
Their Finest Hour (1949)
The Grand Alliance (1950)
The Hinge of Fate (1950)
Closing the Ring (1951)
Triumph and Tragedy (1953)

Poetical Feet

The groups of syllables that make up a unit of verse.

ANAPEST......................two unaccented syllables, one accented

DACTYL........................one accented, two unaccented

IAMB............................one unaccented, one accented

PYRRHIC......................two unaccented

SPONDEE.....................two accented

TROCHEE.....................one accented, one unaccented

Santa's Reindeer

In the order introduced by Clement Moore in his poem "A Visit From St. Nicholas". It was first published in the *Troy Sentinel* (a New York newspaper) on December 23, 1823.

Dasher
Dancer
Prancer
Vixen
Comet
Cupid
Donder
Blitzen

"Donder" and "Blitzen" are the German words for thunder and lightning, respectively.

Carl Sandburg's Chicago Nicknames

In the order mentioned in his 1916 poem "Chicago."

Hog Butcher for the World
Tool Maker
Stacker of Wheat
Player with Railroads
The Nation's Freight Handler
City of the Big Shoulders

Mythical Multipart Animals

CENTAUR....... body of a horse; head and upper torso of a man

CHIMERA....... head of a lion; body of a goat; tail of a serpent

FAUN............ upper body of a man; ears, horns, tail and legs of a goat

GRIFFIN........ body of a lion; head and wings of an eagle

HARPY.......... head of a woman; body of a bird

MANTICORE... body of a lion; head of a man; tail of a dragon (or scorpion)

MINOTAUR..... body of a man; head of a bull

SPHINX......... body of a lion; wings of an eagle; head of a woman

Giants From Mythology, Fiction and Folklore

Argus (Greek mythology)
Atlas (Greek mythology)
Paul Bunyan (American folklore)
Cronus (Greek mythology)
Cyclops (Greek mythology)
Gargantua (Rabelais)
Goliath (Old Testament)
Hyperion (Greek mythology)
Oceanus (Greek mythology)
Orion (Greek mythology)
Pantagruel (Rabelais)
Polyphemus (Greek mythology)
Prometheus (Greek mythology)
Rhea (Greek mythology)
windigo (American Indian folklore)
Ymir (Norse mythology)

Magazines' First Issues

American Heritage ....September 1949

Atlantic Monthly ....November 1857

Boys' Life ....March 1911

Business Week ....September 7, 1929

Consumer Reports ....May 1936

Cosmopolitan ....March 1886

Discover ....October 1980

Ebony ....November 1945

Esquire ....Autumn 1933

Field and Stream ....August 1873

Fortune ....February 1930

Games ....September/October 1977

Good Housekeeping ....May 2, 1885

Gourmet ....January 1941

Harper's ....June 1850

Highlights for Children ....June 1946

Jack and Jill ....November 1938

Junior Scholastic ....September 18, 1937

Ladies' Home Journal ....December 1883

Life ....November 23, 1936 (cover: Fort Peck Dam, Montana)

Look ....January 1937

Mad ....October/November 1952

McCall's ....September 1897

Money ....October 1972

Motor Trend ....September 1949

Ms. ....July 1972

The Nation ....July 6, 1865

National Geographic ....October 1888

National Lampoon ....April 1970

New York ....April 8, 1968

The New Yorker ....February 21, 1925

Newsweek ....February 17, 1933

Omni ....October 1978

People ....March 4, 1974 (cover: Mia Farrow)

Playboy ....December 1953 (cover: Marilyn Monroe)

Playgirl ....January 1973

Popular Science ....May 1872

Premiere ....July/August 1987 (cover: Dan Aykroyd and Tom Hanks)

Psychology Today ....May 1967

Reader's Digest ....February 1922

Redbook..............................September 1903

Road and Track ....June 1947

Rolling Stone.....................November 9, 1967 (cover: John Lennon)

Saturday Evening Post......August 5, 1821

Scientific American ....August 28, 1845

Smithsonian........................April 1970

Spin ....May 1985 (cover: Madonna)

Sport..................................September 1946 (cover: Joe DiMaggio and Joe DiMaggio, Jr.)

The Sporting News ....March 17, 1886

Sports Illustrated ....August 16, 1954 (cover: Ed Mathews)

Sunset ....May 1898

Time ....March 3, 1923 (cover: Joseph G. Cannon, Republican congressman from Illinois)

TV Guide ....April 3, 1953 (cover: Desiderio Alberto Arnaz IV [a.k.a. Desi Arnaz, Jr.] and Lucille Ball)

Us ....May 3, 1977
(cover: Paul Newman)

Variety ....December 16, 1905

Vogue ....December 17, 1892

Woman's Day ....October 7, 1937

Scientific American *is the oldest continuously published magazine in the U.S.*

Dewey Decimal System Major Categories

As conceived by Melvil Dewey and first published in 1876.

000....Generalities
100....Philosophy
200....Religion
300....Social Sciences
400....Languages
500....Pure Sciences
600....Applied Sciences and Technology
700....Arts
800....Literature
900....History and Geography

Sports, Games *and* Toys

Popular Video Games (with U.S. debut dates)

Pong (1972)
Space Invaders (1978)
Asteroids (1979)
Flight Simulator (1979)
Pac-Man (1980)
Donkey Kong (1981)
Super Mario Bros. (1985)
Tetris (1988)
SimCity (1989)
Sonic the Hedgehog (1991)
Mortal Kombat (1992)
Myst (1993)
Doom (1993)
Tomb Raider (1996)
Pokémon (1998)
The Sims (2000)
Halo (2001)

Pac-Man Ghosts

Inky • Blinky • Pinky • Clyde

Magic 8-Ball Messages

The 20 answers found on the icosahedron (20-sided figure) inside.

As I see it, yes.
Ask again later.
Better not tell you now.
Cannot predict now.
Concentrate and ask again.
Don't count on it.
It is certain.
It is decidedly so.
Most likely.
My reply is no.
My sources say no.
Outlook good.
Outlook not so good.
Reply hazy, try again.
Signs point to yes.
Very doubtful.
Without a doubt.
Yes.
Yes—definitely.
You may rely on it.

Tarot Cards

Major Arcana (22)

The Chariot • Death • The Devil • The Emperor • The Empress • The Fool • The Hanged Man • The Hermit • The Hierophant (interpreter of sacred mysteries) • The High Priestess • Judgement [sic] • Justice • The Lovers • The Magician • The Moon • The Star • Strength • The Sun • Temperance • The Tower • Wheel of Fortune • The World

Cups (14)

Ace, 2 through 10, Page, Knight, Queen, King

Pentacles (14)

Ace, 2 through 10, Page, Knight, Queen, King

Swords (14)

Ace, 2 through 10, Page, Knight, Queen, King

Wands (14)

Ace, 2 through 10, Page, Knight, Queen, King

Poker Hands and Odds

Listed below from highest to lowest, with the odds against being dealt each hand in a five-card game.

Royal flush
(649,740 to 1)

Straight flush
(72,193 to 1)

Four of a kind
(4,165 to 1)

Full house
(694 to 1)

Flush
(509 to 1)

Straight
(255 to 1)

Three of a kind
(47 to 1)

Two pair
(21 to 1)

One pair
(2.4 to 1)

No pair
(2 to 1)

Billiard-Ball Colors

Cue ball
white

1 ball
yellow

2 ball
blue

3 ball
red

4 ball
purple

5 ball
orange

6 ball
green

7 ball
plum (dark purple)

8 ball
black

9 ball
white with yellow stripe

10 ball
white with blue stripe

11 ball
white with red stripe

12 ball
white with purple stripe

13 ball
white with orange stripe

14 ball
white with green stripe

15 ball
white with plum stripe

First Beanie Babies

The first nine introduced by Ty Warner in 1993.

Brownie the Bear
Chocolate the Moose
Flash the Dolphin
Legs the Frog
Patti the Platypus
Pinchers the Lobster
Splash the Whale
Spot the Dog
Squealer the Pig

Player Tokens in Monopoly (Standard Version)

battleship • cannon • dog • horse and rider • iron • racecar • sack of money • shoe • thimble • top hat • wheelbarrow

Playing Pieces in Operation

Removing these 13 (mostly plastic) pieces from a toon body is the object of this electric game.

Adam's apple (apple)
The ankle bone's connected to the knee bone (rubber band)
Brain freeze (ice cream cone) *
Bread basket (bread slice)
Broken heart
Butterflies in the stomach (butterfly)

* Introduced October, 2004

Charley horse (horse)
Funny bone
Spare ribs
Water on the knee (pail)
Wish bone
Wrenched ankle (wrench)
Writer's cramp (pencil)

Clue Suspects, Weapons and Rooms

As featured in the standard edition of the whodunit board game. Clue was invented by Englishman Anthony Pratt in 1944.

Suspects (6)

Mr. Green (green token)
Colonel Mustard (yellow token)
Mrs. Peacock (blue token)
Professor Plum (purple token)
Miss Scarlet (red token)
Mrs. White (white token)
(the victim's name is Mr. Boddy)

Weapons (6)

Candlestick
Knife
Lead pipe
Revolver

Rope
Wrench

Rooms (9)
Ballroom
Billiard room
Conservatory
Dining Room
Hall
Kitchen
Library
Lounge
Study

There are a total of 324 possible solutions to the standard edition of the game (6 suspects x 6 weapons x 9 rooms).

Olympic Mascots

• **Summer Games** •

1972 (Munich): Waldi, a dachshund

1976 (Montreal): Amik, a beaver

1980 (Moscow): Misha, a bear

1984 (Los Angeles): Sam, an eagle

1988 (Seoul): Hodori, a tiger cub

1992 (BARCELONA): Cobi, a mountain sheepdog with human shape

1996 (ATLANTA): Izzy, a biologically unidentifiable toon*

2000 (SYDNEY): Syd, a platypus; Millie, an echidna; Olly, a kookaburra

2004 (ATHENS): Phevos and Athena (cartoon children)

• **WINTER GAMES** •

1976 (INNSBRUCK): Schneemandl, a Tyrolean snowman

1980 (LAKE PLACID): Roni, a raccoon

1984 (SARAJEVO): Vucko, a wolf

1988 (CALGARY): Hidy and Howdy, bears

1992 (ALBERTVILLE): Magique, an animated Savoyard star

1994 (LILLEHAMMER): Haakon and Kristin, Norwegian folk-character children

1998 (NAGANO): Sukki, Nokki, Lekki and Tsukki the Snowlets (baby owls)

2002 (SALT LAKE CITY): Powder (snowshoe hare), Copper (coyote), Coal (American black bear)

* IZZY IS SHORT FOR "WHATIZIT"

Auto-Racing Flags

Green	start
Red	stop
Yellow	caution
Black	leave the track
Blue with yellow diagonal stripe	move to the outside
White	one lap to go
Checkered	finish

"How to Stay Young"

Popularized by "ageless" Hall of Fame baseball pitcher Satchel Paige, and inscribed in its entirety on his tombstone.

1. Avoid fried meats which angry up the blood.
2. If your stomach disputes you, lie down and pacify it with cool thoughts.
3. Keep the juices flowing by jangling around gently as you move.
4. Go very light in the vices, such as carrying on in society. The social ramble ain't restful.
5. Avoid running at all times.
6. Don't look back. Something might be gaining on you.

"Black Sox"

Nickname of eight Chicago White Sox who were permanently banned from professional baseball for their role in "fixing" the outcome of the 1919 World Series.

Eddie Cicotte (pitcher)
Oscar "Happy" Felsch (outfielder)
Arnold "Chick" Gandil (first baseman)
"Shoeless" Joe Jackson (left fielder)
Fred McMullin (pinch hitter)
Charles "Swede" Risberg (shortstop)
George "Buck" Weaver (third baseman)
Claude "Lefty" Williams (pitcher)

Boxing Weight Classes

The maximums within each class.

Minimumweight, a.k.a. Strawweight **(105)**
Junior Flyweight, a.k.a. Light Flyweight **(108)**
Flyweight **(112)**
Junior Bantamweight, a.k.a. Super Flyweight **(115)**
Bantamweight **(118)**
Junior Featherweight, a.k.a. Super Bantamweight **(122)**
Featherweight **(126)**
Junior Lightweight, a.k.a. Super Featherweight **(130)**
Lightweight **(135)**

Junior Welterweight, a.k.a. Super Lightweight (**140**)
Welterweight (**147**)
Junior Middleweight, a.k.a. Super Welterweight (**154**)
Middleweight (**160**)
Super Middleweight (**168**)
Light Heavyweight (**175**)
Cruiserweight, a.k.a. Junior Heavyweight (**190**)
Heavyweight (**NO MAXIMUM**)

UNUSUAL COLLEGE TEAM NICKNAMES

ANTEATERS ....University of California-Irvine

ARMADILLOS ....Our Lady of the Lake University (Texas)

ARTICHOKES................Scottsdale Community College (Arizona)

BANANA SLUGS...........University of California–Santa Cruz

BILLIKENS ....St. Louis University

BLOODHOUNDS ....John Jay College of Criminal Justice (New York)

BONNIES ....St. Bonaventure (New York)

CHANTICLEERS............Coastal Carolina University (South Carolina)

CLAIM JUMPERS ....Columbia College (California)

Dirtbags ....California State-Long Beach (baseball team)

Fighting Koalas ....Columbia College (South Carolina)

Fighting Okra ....Delta State (Mississippi)

Gentlemen ....Centenary (Louisiana)

Gorloks ....Webster University (Missouri)

Hardrockers.............South Dakota School of Mines and Technology

Hatters.....................Stetson

Hokies.......................Virginia Tech

Hoyas.........................Georgetown (Washington, D.C.)

Jaspers......................Manhattan College (New York)

Jumbos ....Tufts (Massachusetts)

Keelhaulers..............California Maritime Academy

Lamps.........................American Baptist College (Tennessee)

Magicians ....Lemoyne-Owen College (Tennessee)

Mastodons ....Indiana-Purdue Fort Wayne

Medics ....Thomas Jefferson University (Pennsylvania)

NANOOKS....................University of Alaska-Fairbanks

POETS.........................Whittier

PROPHETS..................Oklahoma Baptist College

SHOCKERS..................Wichita State

SYCAMORES................Indiana State

TROLLS......................Trinity Christian College (Illinois)

ZIPS..........................University of Akron

TRAVEL

Offbeat Museums

A sampling of American museums devoted to unusual topics, and where to find them.

Angels ....Beloit, Wisconsin

Asphalt ....Rohnert Park, California

Bad Art ....Dedham, Massachusetts

Baking ....Manhattan, Kansas

Bananas ....Auburn, Washington

Barbed Wire ....Lacrosse, Kansas

Bathroom Fixtures ...Worcester, Massachusetts

Fasteners ....Julian, California

Gourds ....Angier, North Carolina

Mustard....................Mount Horeb, Wisconsin

PEZ Dispensers.........Burlingame, California

Sand ....Freeport, Maine

Sandpaper.................Two Harbors, Minnesota

Sewing Machines.......Arlington, Texas

Snowmobiles............Sayner, Wisconsin

SPAM.........................Austin, Minnesota

Superman..................Metropolis, Illinois

SURFING......................Santa Cruz, California

TELEPHONES...............Leslie, Georgia

THERMOMETERS..........Onset, Massachusetts

UFOS.........................Roswell, New Mexico

VACUUM CLEANERS......North Canton, Ohio

VOODOO......................New Orleans, Louisiana

WHISKEY HISTORY.......Bardstown, Kentucky

WOODEN NICKELS........San Antonio, Texas

NONATHLETIC HALLS OF FAME

Many of these have Internet Web sites where one can find additional information, such as a list of their members.

ACCOUNTING...............Columbus, Ohio (fisher.osu.edu/acctmis/hall)

ADVERTISING..............Washington, D.C. (www.aaf.org/awards/ahof.html)

AGRICULTURE..............Banner Springs, Kansas (www.aghalloffame.com)

(GREAT) AMERICANS....Bronx, New York (www.bcc.cuny.edu/halloffame)

ASTRONAUTS...............Titusville, Florida

AUTOMOTIVE ....Dearborn, Michigan (www.automotivehalloffame.org)

AVIATION ....Dayton, Ohio (www.nationalaviation.org)

BURLESQUE ....Helendale, California

CAR COLLECTORS.........Nashville, Tennessee

CHECKERS ....Petal, Mississippi

CHESS........................Washington, D.C. (www.chesslinks.org/hof)

CIRCUS.......................Peru, Indiana (www.circushalloffame.com)

CLASSICAL MUSIC ....Cincinnati, Ohio (www.americanclassicalmusic.org)

CLOWNS ....Milwaukee, Wisconsin (www.theclownmuseum.org)

COMEDY ....St. Petersburg, Florida (www.comedyhall.com)

COUNTRY MUSIC ....Nashville, Tennessee (www.countrymusichalloffame.com)

COWGIRLS ....Fort Worth, Texas (www.cowgirl.net)

ECOLOGY ....Santa Cruz, California (www.ecotopia.org)

(OLDTIME) FIDDLERS ...Weiser, Idaho

HAMBURGERS..............Seymour, Wisconsin

HOT DOGS....................Fairfield, California

INVENTORS ....Akron, Ohio
(www.invent.org)

JEWISH-AMERICANS .....Berkeley, California
(amuseum.org/jahf)

NURSES.......................Washington, D.C.
(www.nursingworld.org/hof)

POLICE........................Titusville, Florida
(www.aphf.org)

QUILTERS ....Marion, Indiana
(www.quiltershalloffame.org)

PHOTOGRAPHY.............Oklahoma City, Oklahoma (www.iphf.org)

RIVERS........................Dubuque, Iowa
(www.mississippirivermuseum.com/nrhf.htm)

ROCK AND ROLL...........Cleveland, Ohio
(www.rockhall.com)

(ROTTEN) SNEAKERS
"HALL OF FUMES" ....Montpelier, Vermont

SONGWRITERS.............New York, New York
(www.songwritershalloffame.org)

(NASHVILLE) SONGWRITERS Nashville, Tennessee
(www.nashvillesongwritersfoundation.com)

SPACE ....Alamogordo, New Mexico (www.spacefame.org)

(HOLLYWOOD) STUNTMEN ....Moab, Utah

(NATIONAL) TEACHERS...Emporia, Kansas (www.nthf.org)

(NATIONAL) WOMEN.....Seneca Falls, New York (www.greatwomen.org)

"WORLD'S LARGEST" ROADSIDE ATTRACTIONS

A sampling of many such self-proclaimed man-made giants throughout the United States.

ALLIGATOR: Christmas, Florida—200 feet long

BASEBALL BAT: Louisville, Kentucky—120 feet high, 68,000 pounds

CHERRY PIE: George, Washington(!)—containing 400 pounds of cherries, baked every July 4th

CHEST OF DRAWERS: High Point, North Carolina —32 feet high

CHICKEN: Marietta, Georgia—55 feet high

CROW: Belgrade, Michigan—18 feet high

CRYSTAL BALL: Westerville, Ohio—700 pounds

CUCKOO CLOCK: Wilmot, Ohio—23.5 feet high

DIXIE CUP: Lexington, Kentucky—9 feet high, 1,360-gallon capacity

FIRE HYDRANT: Beaumont, Texas—24 feet high

GLOBE: Yarmouth, Maine—41 feet in diameter

HARP (PLAYABLE): Santa Fe, New Mexico—13 feet high

HORSE: Grand Rapids, Michigan—28 feet long, 24 feet high, 27,000 pounds

ICOSAHEDRON (SOLID FIGURE WITH 20 FACES): Lexington, Massachusetts—15 feet high

KALEIDOSCOPE: Mt. Tremper, New York—60 feet high

KETCHUP BOTTLE: Collinsville, Illinois—170 feet high

OFFICE CHAIR: Anniston, Alabama—33 feet high

PORCH SWING: Hebron, Nebraska—32 feet long

POTATO CHIP: Blackfoot, Idaho—25 inches by 14 inches

RUBBER STAMP: Cleveland, Ohio—48 feet long (it reads "FREE")

STOVE: Detroit, Michigan—25 feet high

STRAWBERRY: Strawberry Point, Iowa—12 feet high

Teapot: Chester, West Virginia—14 feet high

Thermometer: Baker, California ("Gateway to Death Valley")—134 feet high, in honor of the 134 degree temperature recorded in Death Valley in 1913

Weather vane: White Lake, Michigan—48 feet high

U.S. "Capitals" of the World

A sampling of the many such self-created "official" nicknames of tourist attractions.

Artichoke ....Castroville, California

Blueberry ....Cherryfield, Maine

Bluebird...................Bickleton, Washington

Carpet ....Dalton, Georgia

Chili ....Hatch, New Mexico

Christmas Tree.........Indiana County, Pennsylvania

Coaster ....Cedar Point Amusement Park, Sandusky, Ohio (home of 14 roller coasters, more than anywhere else in the world)

Copper......................Kearny, Arizona

Covered Bridge ....Parke County, Indiana (home of 32 covered bridges)

Entertainment ....Las Vegas, Nevada

Folk Music ....Mountain View, Arkansas

Frog ....Rayne, Louisiana

Furniture ....High Point, North Carolina

Garlic........................Gilroy, California

Halibut Fishing.........Homer, Alaska

Hog............................Kewanee, Illinois

Honey ....Uvalde, Texas

Horse ....Lexington, Kentucky

Horseradish ....Collinsville, Illinois

Ice Cream...................Le Mars, Iowa (home of Blue Bunny ice cream)

Killer Bee.................Hidalgo, Texas (where killer bees first entered the U.S. in 1990)

Media.........................Burbank, California

Pottery......................Marshall, Texas

Poultry ....Georgia (by legislative act)

Quartz Crystal ....Mount Ida, Arkansas

Scarecrow................Walton, New York

Shark Tooth..............Venice, Florida

Sock...........................Fort Payne, Alabama

Soybean ....Decatur, Illinois

Submarine ....Groton, Connecticut

Watermelon..............Cordele, Georgia

Boeing Passenger Planes

Numerical designations, nicknames (if any) and the years that the planes first flew.

40: 1925
80: 1928
247: 1933
307 "Stratoliner": 1938
314 "Clipper": 1938
377 "Stratocruiser": 1947
707: 1954
720: 1959
727: 1963
737: 1967
747: 1969
767: 1981
757: 1982
777: 1994
717: 1995
787 "Dreamliner": first flight planned for 2007

Goodyear Blimps

The first Goodyear blimp was the *Pilgrim,* built in 1925. There are currently three blimps in the Goodyear U.S. corporate fleet:

Spirit of Goodyear (Akron, Ohio)
Eagle (Carson, California)
Stars and Stripes (Pompano Beach, Florida)

Major Cities on Route 66

Route 66 was one of America's major east-west highways from the 1940s to the 1960s.

Chicago, Illinois
St. Louis, Missouri
Springfield, Missouri
Tulsa, Oklahoma
Oklahoma City, Oklahoma
Amarillo, Texas
Albuquerque, New Mexico
Flagstaff, Arizona
Los Angeles, California

Major "Named" U.S. Airports

Atlanta, Georgia.......Hartsfield International

Boston, Massachusetts..........Logan International

Charleston, West Virginia............Yeager

Chicago, Illinois.......Midway, O'Hare International

Cleveland, Ohio........Hopkins International

Houston, Texas.........George Bush Intercontinental, Hobby

KNOXVILLE, TENNESSEE.................McGhee Tyson

LAS VEGAS, NEVADA.....McCarran International

LEXINGTON, KENTUCKY..Blue Grass

MILWAUKEE, WISCONSIN.................Mitchell International

NEW YORK, NEW YORK...La Guardia International, John F. Kennedy International

NEW ORLEANS, LOUISIANA..................Louis Armstrong International

OKLAHOMA CITY, OKLAHOMA..................Will Rogers World Airport

ORANGE COUNTY, CALIFORNIA (SANTA ANA)..............John Wayne

PHOENIX, ARIZONA.......Sky Harbor International

ST. LOUIS, MISSOURI...Lambert International

SAN DIEGO, CALIFORNIA................Lindbergh Field

SAN JUAN, PUERTO RICO..............Luis Muñoz Marin International

WASHINGTON, D.C.........Dulles, Ronald Reagan Washington National

MAJOR "NAMED" WORLD AIRPORTS

AMSTERDAM, NETHERLANDS ....Schipol

ATHENS, GREECE ....Ellinikon

BERLIN, GERMANY ....Tegel

BRNO, CZECH REPUBLIC ....Turany

BUDAPEST, HUNGARY ...Ferihegi

BUENOS AIRES, ARGENTINA ....Ezeiza

CALCUTTA, INDIA..........Dum Dum

CARACAS, VENEZUELA...Simón Bolívar International

CASABLANCA, MOROCCO ....Mohammed V International

COPENHAGEN, DENMARK ....Kastrup

FLORENCE, ITALY ....Amerigo Vespucci

GENOA, ITALY ....Christopher Columbus

GDAŃSK, POLAND.........Lech Walesa

HAVANA, CUBA............José Martí International

HONG KONG, CHINA......Chek Lap Kok

ISTANBUL, TURKEY.......Ataturk

LISBON, PORTUGAL ......Portela

LONDON, ENGLAND.......Gatwick, Heathrow

MADRID, SPAIN ....Barajas

MANILA, PHILIPPINES ...Ninoy Aquino International

MELBOURNE,
AUSTRALIA..................Tullamarine International

MEXICO CITY, MEXICO...Benito Juárez International

MONTREAL, CANADA .....Mirabel

MOSCOW, RUSSIA.........Sheremetyevo International

NAIROBI, KENYA ....Jomo Kenyatta International

NEW DELHI, INDIA........Indira Gandhi International

NICE, FRANCE.............Côte d'Azur

OSLO, NORWAY ....Gardermoen International

PARIS, FRANCE ....Charles de Gaulle, Orly

PISA, ITALY ....Galileo Galilei

PRAGUE,
CZECH REPUBLIC ....Ruzyne

RIO DE JANEIRO,
BRAZIL........................Galeão International

ROME, ITALY ....Fiumicino (Leonardo da Vinci)

ST. MAARTEN, NETHERLANDS
ANTILLES.....................Princess Juliana International

SEOUL, SOUTH KOREA...Kimpo International

SINGAPORE.................Changi

STOCKHOLM, SWEDEN...Arlanda

SYDNEY, AUSTRALIA.....Kingsford Smith

TAIPEI, TAIWAN...........Chiang Kai-shek International

TEL AVIV, ISRAEL.........Ben-Gurion International

TOKYO, JAPAN.............Narita International

TORONTO, CANADA.......Lester B. Pearson International

VENICE, ITALY.............Marco Polo

VIENNA, AUSTRIA.........Schwechat

WARSAW, POLAND........Okecie

AMERICA

U.S. Presidents Who Never Attended College

George Washington
Andrew Jackson
Martin Van Buren
Zachary Taylor
Millard Fillmore
Abraham Lincoln
Andrew Johnson
Grover Cleveland
Harry S Truman

Four Freedoms

As presented in a speech delivered to a joint session of Congress by President Franklin D. Roosevelt on January 6, 1941.

Freedom of speech and expression
Freedom of worship
Freedom from want
Freedom from fear

LINCOLN-DOUGLAS DEBATE SITES

Senatorial candidates Abraham Lincoln and Stephen Douglas visited these seven Illinois cities in their historic debates of 1858.

OTTAWA ....August 21
FREEPORT ....August 27
JONESBORO..........September 15
CHARLESTON ....September 18
GALESBURG..........October 7
QUINCY................October 13
ACTON ....October 15

BILL OF RIGHTS SUBJECTS

These first ten amendments to the U.S. Constitution took effect on December 15, 1791.

FIRST AMENDMENT.......Freedom of religion, freedom of speech, freedom of the press, right to assemble peaceably, right to petition the Government

SECOND AMENDMENT ...Right to keep and bear arms

THIRD AMENDMENT......Quartering of soldiers

FOURTH AMENDMENT....Unreasonable search and seizure

FIFTH AMENDMENT.......Grand juries, double jeopardy, testifying against oneself, private property taken for public use

Sixth Amendment ......Speedy trial, impartial jury, obtaining witnesses

Seventh Amendment ..Right of trial by jury

Eighth Amendment ....Excessive bail/fines, cruel and unusual punishment

Ninth Amendment ......Rights retained by the people

Tenth Amendment......Rights retained by the States

U.S. Coins Vital Statistics

Diameter

Penny: .75 inches (19.05 millimeters)

Nickel: .835 inches (21.21 millimeters)

Dime: .705 inches (17.91 millimeters)

Quarter: .955 inches (24.26 millimeters)

Half Dollar: 1.205 inches (30.61 millimeters)

Sacagawea Dollar: 1.043 inches (26.5 millimeters)

Number of Coins in a One-Foot Stack

Pennies: 197

Nickels: 156

Dimes: 226

Quarters: 174

Half Dollars: 142

Sacagawea Dollars: 152

Number of Coins Per Pound

Pennies: 181

Nickels: 91

Dimes: 200

Quarters: 80

Half Dollars: 40

Sacagawea Dollars: 56

Thickness

Penny: .061 inches (1.55 millimeters)

Nickel: .077 inches (1.95 millimeters)

Dime: .053 inches (1.35 millimeters)

Quarter: .069 inches (1.75 millimeters)

Half Dollar: .085 inches (2.15 millimeters)

Sacagawea Dollar: .079 inches (2 millimeters)

Weight

Penny: .088 ounces (2.5 grams)

Nickel: .176 ounces (5 grams)

Dime: .08 ounces (2.268 grams)

Quarter: .2 ounces (5.67 grams)

Half Dollar: .4 ounces (11.34 grams)

Sacagawea Dollar: .286 ounces (8.1 grams)

Ivy League Schools

Listed below with their founding dates.

Brown University (1764)
Columbia University (1754)
Cornell University (1865)
Dartmouth University (1769)
Harvard University (1636)
University of Pennsylvania (1740)
Princeton University (1746)
Yale University (1701)

Rivers of U.S. State Capitals and Major Cities

State capitals not listed are not located on a river.

Albany, New York
Hudson

Albuquerque, New Mexico
Rio Grande

Annapolis, Maryland
Severn

Augusta, Maine
Kennebec

Austin, Texas
Colorado

Baltimore, Maryland
Patapsco

Baton Rouge, Louisiana
Mississippi

Bismarck, North Dakota
Missouri

Boise, Idaho
Boise

Boston, Massachusetts
Charles, Mystic

Charleston, West Virginia
Elk, Kanawha

Cheyenne, Wyoming
Crow Creek

Chicago, Illinois
Chicago

Cincinnati, Ohio
Ohio

Cleveland, Ohio
Cuyahoga

Colorado Springs, Colorado
Monument Creek, Fountain Creek

Columbia, South Carolina
Congaree

Columbus, Ohio
Scioto

Concord, New Hampshire
Merrimack

Dallas, Texas
Trinity

Denver, Colorado
South Platte

Des Moines, Iowa
Des Moines, Raccoon

Detroit, Michigan
Detroit

El Paso, Texas
Rio Grande

Fort Worth, Texas
Trinity

Frankfort, Kentucky
Kentucky

Harrisburg, Pennsylvania
Susquehanna

Hartford, Connecticut
Connecticut

Indianapolis, Indiana
White

Jackson, Mississippi
Pearl

Jacksonville, Florida
St. Johns

Jefferson City, Missouri
Missouri

Kansas City, Missouri
Missouri

Lansing, Michigan
Grand, Red Cedar

Little Rock, Arkansas
Arkansas

Memphis, Tennessee
Mississippi

Miami, Florida
Miami

Milwaukee, Wisconsin
Milwaukee, Menomonee, Kinnickinnic

Minneapolis, Minnesota
Mississippi

Montgomery, Alabama
Alabama

Montpelier, Vermont
Winooski

Nashville, Tennessee
Cumberland

New York, New York
Hudson, East, Harlem

Oklahoma City, Oklahoma
North Canadian

Omaha, Nebraska
Missouri

Philadelphia, Pennsylvania
Delaware, Schuylkill

Phoenix, Arizona
Salt

Pierre, South Dakota
Missouri

Pittsburgh, Pennsylvania
Allegheny, Monongahela, Ohio

Portland, Oregon
Willamette

Providence, Rhode Island
Providence

Richmond, Virginia
James

Sacramento, California
Sacramento

St. Louis, Missouri
Mississippi

St. Paul, Minnesota
Mississippi

Salem, Oregon
Willamette

Salt Lake City, Utah
Jordan

San Antonio, Texas
San Antonio

San Jose, California
Coyote, Guadalupe

Springfield, Illinois
Sangamon

Topeka, Kansas
Kansas

Trenton, New Jersey
Delaware

Tucson, Arizona
Santa Cruz

Tulsa, Oklahoma
Arkansas

Washington, D.C.
Potomac, Anacostia

Most Popular County Names

The county names (including parish names in Louisiana) used by the most states.

Washington (31 states)
Jefferson (26)
Franklin (24)
Jackson (24)
Lincoln (24)
Madison (20)
Montgomery (18)
Union (18)
Clay (17)
Marion (17)
Monroe (17)

Six Flags Over Texas Flags

Arlington, Texas amusement park, the first in the Six Flags chain, opened in 1961. It is named for the six national flags that have flown over Texas.

Spain
France
Mexico
Republic of Texas (the current Texas state flag)
Confederate States of America
United States

Stars and Stripes on the U.S. Flag

Each star on the American flag represents a state of the Union. Since 1795, new stars have been added as new states have been admitted.

13 STARS: 1777—1795 (original 13 colonies)

15 STARS: 1795—1818 (Vermont, Kentucky)

20 STARS: 1818—July 3, 1819 (Tennessee, Ohio, Louisiana, Indiana, Mississippi)

21 STARS: July 4, 1819—July 3, 1820 (Illinois)

23 STARS: July 4, 1820—July 3, 1822 (Alabama, Maine)

24 STARS: July 4, 1822—July 3, 1836 (Missouri)

25 STARS: July 4, 1836—July 3, 1837 (Arkansas)

26 STARS: July 4, 1837—July 3, 1845 (Michigan)

27 STARS: July 4, 1845—July 3, 1846 (Florida)

28 STARS: July 4, 1846—July 3, 1847 (Texas)

29 STARS: July 4, 1847—July 3, 1848 (Iowa)

30 STARS: July 4, 1848—July 3, 1851 (Wisconsin)

31 STARS: July 4, 1851—July 3, 1858 (California)

32 STARS: July 4, 1858—July 3, 1859 (Minnesota)

33 STARS: July 4, 1859—July 3, 1861 (Oregon)

34 STARS: July 4, 1861—July 3, 1863 (Kansas)

35 STARS: July 4, 1863—July 3, 1865 (West Virginia)

36 STARS: July 4, 1865—July 3, 1867 (Nevada)

37 STARS: July 4, 1867—July 3, 1877 (Nebraska)

38 STARS: July 4, 1877—July 3, 1890 (Colorado)

43 STARS: July 4, 1890—July 3, 1891 (North Dakota, South Dakota, Montana, Washington, Idaho)

44 STARS: July 4, 1891—July 3, 1896 (Wyoming)

45 STARS: July 4, 1896—July 3, 1908 (Utah)

46 STARS: July 4, 1908—July 3, 1912 (Oklahoma)

48 STARS: July 4, 1912—July 3, 1959 (New Mexico, Arizona)

49 STARS: July 4, 1959—July 3, 1960 (Alaska)

50 STARS: July 4, 1960—present (Hawaii)

At first, each stripe on the American flag represented a state of the Union. In 1818, this was changed back by Congress to the fixed number of 13, to represent the original 13 colonies.

13 STRIPES: 1777–1795

15 STRIPES: 1795–1818 (Vermont, Kentucky)

13 STRIPES: 1818 to present

Where the American Flag Is Flown Continuously

By presidential proclamation, the American flag is flown 24 hours a day at these sites:

Flag House Square, Baltimore, Maryland
Fort McHenry, Baltimore, Maryland
Town Green, Lexington, Massachusetts
U.S. Marine Corps Memorial
(a.k.a. Iwo Jima Memorial), Arlington, Virginia
Valley Forge National Memorial, Valley Forge, Pennsylvania
Washington Monument, Washington, D.C.
The White House, Washington, D.C.

UNITED STATES NATIONAL CAPITALS

The cities that have served as capitals of the United States (by definition, where Congress has met), from the First Continental Congress to the present.

SEPTEMBER 1774 TO DECEMBER 1776
Philadelphia, Pennsylvania

DECEMBER 1776 TO MARCH 1777
Baltimore, Maryland

MARCH 1777 TO SEPTEMBER 1777
Philadelphia

SEPTEMBER 1777
Lancaster, Pennsylvania

SEPTEMBER 1777 TO JULY 1778
York, Pennsylvania

JULY 1778 TO JUNE 1783
Philadelphia

June 1783 to November 1783
Trenton, New Jersey

November 1783 to January 1785
Annapolis, Maryland

January 1785 to July 1790
New York, New York

July 1790 to October 1800
Philadelphia

October 1800 to present
Washington, D.C.

Honorary Citizens of the United States

Sir Winston Churchill (1963)
Raoul Wallenberg (1981)
William and Hannah Penn (1984)
Mother Teresa (1996)

The Marquis de Lafayette was made an honorary citizen of several states, but not of the U.S. as a whole.

POSTAL RATES

*H*istory of the effective dates for rate changes in the cost of a first-class letter.

JULY 1, 1863
3 cents

OCTOBER 1, 1863
2 cents

NOVEMBER 3, 1917
3 cents (war emergency rate)

JULY 1, 1919
2 cents

JULY 6, 1932
3 cents

AUGUST 1, 1958
4 cents

JANUARY 7, 1963
5 cents

JANUARY 7, 1968
6 cents

MAY 16, 1971
8 cents

MARCH 2, 1974
10 cents

DECEMBER 31, 1975
13 cents

MAY 29, 1978
15 cents

MARCH 22, 1981
18 cents

NOVEMBER 1, 1981
20 cents

FEBRUARY 17, 1985
22 cents

APRIL 3, 1988
25 cents

FEBRUARY 3, 1991
29 cents

JANUARY 1, 1995
32 cents

JANUARY 1, 1999
33 cents

JANUARY 7, 2001
34 cents

JUNE 30, 2002
37 cents

Prior to 1863, letter rates were based in part on the distance traveled.

Consecutive-Digit Zip Codes

12345 ....Schenectady, New York
23456 ....Virginia Beach, Virginia
45678 ....Scottown, Ohio

Single-Number Zip Codes

22222 ....Arlington, Virginia
44444 ....Newton Falls, Ohio
55555 ....Young America, Minnesota

World Nations *and* History

United Nations Secretaries-General

1946-52: Trygve Halvdan Lie (Norway)

1953-61: Dag Hjalmar Agne Carl Hammarskjöld (Sweden)

1961-71: U Thant (Burma, now known as Myanmar)

1972-81: Kurt Waldheim (Austria)

1982-91: Javier Pérez de Cuellar (Peru)

1992-96: Boutros Boutros-Ghali (Egypt)

1997-Present: Kofi Atta Annan (Ghana)

American diplomat Alger Hiss (who later ran afoul of the House Un-American Activities Committee and California congressman Richard Nixon) served as secretary-general at the U.N. founding conference at San Francisco in 1945, and is sometimes considered to be the first U.N. secretary-general.

Official Languages of South Africa

South Africa's 11 official languages are the most for any country:

> Afrikaans • English • Ndebele • Northern Sotho (a.k.a. Pedi) • Southern Sotho • Swazi • Tsonga • Tswana • Venda • Xhosa • Zulu

India has only two official languages (Hindi and English), but the constitution of India recognizes an additional 18 state languages.

English Monarchs Buried at London's Westminster Abbey

With death dates listed below.

Edward the Confessor (1066)
Henry III (1272)
Edward I (1307)
Edward III (1377)
Richard II (1400)
Henry V (1422)
Edward V (1483)
Henry VII (1509)
Edward VI (1553)
Mary I (1558)

Elizabeth I (1603)
James I (1625)
Charles II (1685)
Mary II (1694)
William III (1702)
Anne (1714)
George II (1760)

Six Wives of Henry VIII

Catherine of Aragón
daughter of Ferdinand and Isabella, mother of Mary I (married 1509, marriage annulled 1533)

Anne Boleyn
mother of Elizabeth I (married 1533, beheaded 1536)

Jane Seymour
mother of Edward VI (married 1536, died 1537)

Anne of Cleves
(married 1540, marriage annulled 1540)

Catherine Howard
(married 1540, beheaded 1542)

Catherine Parr
(married 1543, survived him)

Legion of Honor Classes

French order of military and civil merit created by Napoleon in 1802. Admission requires either 20 years of peacetime civil achievement, or military bravery in wartime. The Legion's five classes, in descending order:

Grand cross
Grand officer
Commander
Officer
Knight

Countries' Former Names

Australia .... New Holland

Bangladesh .... East Pakistan

Belize .... British Honduras

Benin .... Dahomey

Botswana .... Bechuanaland

Burkina Faso .... Upper Volta

Central African Republic ...... Ubangi-Shari

Djibouti .... French Somaliland

Ethiopia .... Abyssinia

GHANA ....Gold Coast

GUYANA.......................British Guiana

INDONESIA..................Dutch East Indies

IRAN ....Persia

JORDAN......................Transjordan

KENYA.........................East Africa Protectorate

LESOTHO ....Basutoland

MALAWI.......................Nyasaland

MALI...........................French Sudan

MOZAMBIQUE.............Portuguese East Africa

MYANMAR..................Burma

NAMIBIA.....................German Southwest Africa

NAURU ....Pleasant Island

SRI LANKA ....Ceylon

SURINAME ....Dutch Guiana

TUVALU ....Ellice Islands

UNITED ARAB EMIRATES ....Trucial States

VANUATU ....New Hebrides

ZAMBIA ....Northern Rhodesia

ZIMBABWE..................Southern Rhodesia

Rivers of Major World Cities

Alexandria, Egypt: Nile

Amsterdam, Netherlands: Amstel

Baghdad, Iraq: Tigris

Bangkok, Thailand: Chao Phraya

Belgrade, Yugoslavia: Danube, Sava

Berlin, Germany: Spree, Havel

Bogotá, Colombia: Bogotá

Brussels, Belgium: Senne

Budapest, Hungary: Danube

Buenos Aires, Argentina: Río de la Plata

Cairo, Egypt: Nile

Calcutta, India: Hugli

Damascus, Syria: Barada

Delhi, India: Yamuna

Dublin, Ireland: Liffey

Ho Chi Minh City, Vietnam: Saigon

Hong Kong, China: Pearl

Jakarta, Indonesia: Liwung

Kiev, Ukraine: Dneiper

Lima, Peru: Rímac

Lisbon, Portugal: Tagus

London, England: Thames

Madrid, Spain: Manzanares

Melbourne, Australia: Yarra

Montreal, Canada: St. Lawrence

Moscow, Russia: Moskva

Paris, France: Seine

Prague, Czech Republic: Moldau

Rome, Italy: Tiber

Saint Petersburg, Russia: Neva

Santiago, Chile: Mapocho

São Paulo, Brazil: Tietê

Seoul, South Korea: Han

Shanghai, China: Huangpu

Tokyo, Japan: Sumida

Vienna, Austria: Danube

Warsaw, Poland: Vistula

Zagreb, Croatia: Sava

Zurich, Switzerland: Limmat, Sihl

Major War-Ending Treaties

Seven Years' War (a.k.a. French and Indian War): Treaty of Paris (1763)

American Revolution: Treaty of Paris (1783)

War of 1812: Treaty of Ghent (1814)

Mexican War: Treaty of Guadalupe Hidalgo (1848)

Crimean War: Treaty of Paris (1856)

Franco-Prussian War: Treaty of Frankfurt (1871)

Spanish-American War: Treaty of Paris (1898)

Boer War: Treaty of Vereeniging (1902)

Russo-Japanese War: Treaty of Portsmouth (1905)

World War I: Treaty of Versailles (1919)

Chinese Zodiac "Year of the" Animals

The next year in the 12-year cycle is given with each animal.

Rat (2008)	Dragon (2012)	Monkey (2016)
Ox (2009)	Snake (2013)	Rooster (2017)
Tiger (2010)	Horse (2014)	Dog (2006)
Rabbit (2011)	Ram (2015)	Pig (2007)

SCIENCE

MODIFIED MERCALLI SCALE

Alternative to the Richter scale for measuring the intensity of earthquakes. Its 1-12 (I-XII) scale is based on the amount of damage caused, rather than the absolute intensity that is measured by the Richter scale. The original scale was devised by Italian geologist Giuseppe Mercalli in 1902; this modified scale was introduced by seismologist Charles F. Richter in 1956.

I.......Barely felt
II......Felt by a small number of people
III ....Slightly felt indoors
IV.....Felt indoors by many people
V......Felt by most people, very minor damage
VI.....Felt by everyone, slight damage
VII....Considerable damage in poorly constructed buildings
VIII ..Heavy damage in poorly constructed buildings
IX.....Considerable damage to well-constructed buildings
X......Most buildings destroyed
XI.....Few buildings left standing
XII....Total destruction

MOHS SCALE

Relative scale for the hardness of minerals, developed by Austrian mineralogist Friedrich Mohs.

1 ...... Talc
2 ...... Gypsum
3 ...... Calcite
4 ...... Fluorite
5 ...... Apatite
6 ...... Orthoclase
7 ...... Quartz
8 ...... Topaz
9 ...... Corundum
10 .... Diamond

FUJITA SCALE

Scale used to measure the intensity of tornadoes.

CATEGORY F0: Gale tornado (40-72 mph). Some damage to chimneys, broken tree branches, shallow-rooted trees pushed over.

CATEGORY F1: Moderate tornado (73-112 mph). Roof surfaces peel, mobile homes pushed off foundations or overturned, moving autos pushed off the road.

Category F2: Significant tornado (113-157 mph). Roofs torn off frame houses, mobile homes demolished, boxcars pushed over, large trees snapped or uprooted.

Category F3: Severe tornado (158-206 mph). Roofs and walls torn off well-constructed houses, trains overturned, heavy cars lifted off the ground.

Category F4: Devastating tornado (207-260 mph). Well-constructed houses leveled, structures with weak foundation moved some distance, cars thrown, large missiles generated.

Category F5: Incredible tornado (261-318 mph). Strong frame houses lifted off foundations and carried considerable distance, car-sized missiles fly through the air more than 100 yards.

Project Mercury Astronauts and Spacecraft

Mercury 3 (1961—Alan Shepard): Freedom 7

Mercury 4 (1961—Virgil Grissom): Liberty Bell 7

Mercury 6 (1962—John Glenn): Friendship 7

Mercury 7 (1962—Scott Carpenter): Aurora 7

Mercury 8 (1962—Wally Schirra): Sigma 7

Mercury 9 (1963—Gordon Cooper): Faith 7

The "7" in each name refers to the seven original Mercury astronauts. Donald "Deke" Slayton was originally scheduled to pilot Mercury 7, but was relieved of his assignment due to a heart condition. Slayton eventually made it into space as the docking-module pilot for the Apollo-Soyuz mission of 1975.

Project Apollo Astronauts and Mission Modules

Command Modules are listed first, followed by the Lunar Modules.

Apollo 9

1969—James McDivitt, David Scott, Russell Schweickart: Gumdrop, Spider

Apollo 10

1969—Thomas Stafford, John Young, Eugene Cernan: Charlie Brown, Snoopy

Apollo 11

1969—Neil Armstrong*, Michael Collins, Buzz Aldrin*: Columbia, Eagle

Apollo 12

1969—Charles Conrad*, Richard Gordon, Alan Bean*: Yankee Clipper, Intrepid

* One of the twelve astronauts to walk on the moon

APOLLO 13

1970—JAMES LOVELL, JOHN SWIGERT, FRED HAISE: Odyssey, Aquarius

APOLLO 14

1971—ALAN SHEPARD*, STUART ROOSA, EDGAR MITCHELL*: Kitty Hawk, Antares

APOLLO 15

1972—DAVID SCOTT*, ALFRED WORDEN, JAMES IRWIN*: Endeavour, Falcon

APOLLO 16

1972—JOHN YOUNG*, THOMAS MATTINGLY, CHARLES DUKE*: Casper, Orion

APOLLO 17

1972—EUGENE CERNAN*, RONALD EVANS, HARRISON SCHMITT*: America, Challenger

CLASSIFICATION OF ROCKS

Listed below with examples of each.

MAGMA......................molten rock (lava)

IGNEOUS....................formed from magma (granite, pumice, basalt)

* ONE OF THE TWELVE ASTRONAUTS TO WALK ON THE MOON

SEDIMENTARY ....formed from the remains of other rocks (sandstone, shale, limestone)

METAMORPHIC.............formed from other rocks by heat and/or pressure (mica, slate, marble)

SINGLE-LETTER CHEMICAL-ELEMENT SYMBOLS

B....boron

C....carbon

F....fluorine

H....hydrogen

I.....iodine

K....potassium

N....nitrogen

O....oxygen

P....phosphorus

S....sulfur

U....uranium

V....vanadium

W...tungsten

Y....yttrium

Vitamin Names and Deficiencies

Vitamins' chemical names, with diseases caused by a deficiency of the vitamins.

A ......retinol (night blindness)
B1 ....thiamine (beriberi)
B2 ....riboflavin
B3 ....niacin, nicotinic acid (pellagra)
B6 ....pyridoxine
B9 ....folic acid
B12 ..cobalamin, cyanocobalamin
C ......ascorbic acid (scurvy)
D ......rickets
E ......tocopherol
K1 ....phylloquinone

Phobias

Some technical terms for abnormal fears:

ACROPHOBIA ....heights

AEROPHOBIA ....drafts

AGORAPHOBIA ....open spaces, crowds, public places

AICHMOPHOBIA............needles

AILUROPHOBIA.............cats

ALGOPHOBIA ....pain

AMBULOPHOBIA ....walking

ANDROPHOBIA ....men

ANGLOPHOBIA ....England, English culture

APHENPHOSMPHOBIA....being touched

APIPHOBIA ....bees

ARACHIBUTYROPHOBIA...peanut butter sticking to the roof of one's mouth

ARACHNOPHOBIA..........spiders

ASTRAPHOBIA..............thunder and lightning

ATYCHIPHOBIA.............failure

AUROPHOBIA ....gold

AUTOMYSOPHOBIA........getting dirty

AVIOPHOBIA ....flying

BATRACHOPHOBIA ....frogs

BIBLIOPHOBIA ....books

CATOPTROPHOBIA.........mirrors

CHIONOPHOBIA ....snow

CHOREOPHOBIA ....dancing

CLAUSTROPHOBIA.........enclosed places

CREMNOPHOBIA...........precipices

CYBERPHOBIA..............working with computers

CYNOPHOBIA ....dogs

DENDROPHOBIA ....trees

DIDASKALEINOPHOBIA...going to school

ECOPHOBIA ....home

ENTOMOPHOBIA ....insects

ERGOPHOBIA ....work

ERYTHROPHOBIA ....red, blushing

FRANCOPHOBIA............France, French culture

GAMOPHOBIA...............marriage

GEPHYROPHOBIA..........crossing bridges

GLOSSOPHOBIA............speaking in public

GYNEPHOBIA ....women

HELIOPHOBIA ....the Sun

HEMOPHOBIA...............blood

HERPETOPHOBIA ....reptiles

HIPPOPHOBIA ....horses

HYDROPHOBIA ....water

IATROPHOBIA ....doctors

ICHTHYOPHOBIA...........fish

LALOPHOBIA................speaking

LOGOPHOBIA ....words

LYSSOPHOBIA..............going insane

MONOPHOBIA ....being alone

MUSOPHOBIA...............mice

MYSOPHOBIA...............dirt

NEOPHOBIA.................new things

NOSOPHOBIA ....disease

NYCTOPHOBIA..............darkness

OCHLOPHOBIA.............crowds

ODONTOPHOBIA ....dentists

OMBROPHOBIA.............rain

OPHIDIOPHOBIA...........snakes

ORNITHOPHOBIA ....birds

PANOPHOBIA ....everything

PATHOPHOBIA..............disease

PECCATOPHOBIA..........sinning

PHILEMAPHOBIA...........kissing

PHOBOPHOBIA ....one's own fears

PHOTOPHOBIA..............light

POGONOPHOBIA ....beards

PSYCHROPHOBIA..........cold

PYROPHOBIA ....fire

SESQUIPEDALOPHOBIA ..long words

SINOPHOBIA................Chinese, Chinese culture

SITOPHOBIA ....food

SPECTROPHOBIA ....ghosts

TAPHEPHOBIA ....being buried alive

THALASSOPHOBIA.........the sea

THANATOPHOBIA ....dying

TOXIPHOBIA ....being poisoned

TRAUMATOPHOBIA ....injury

TRISKAIDEKAPHOBIA.....the number 13

XENOPHOBIA ....strangers, foreigners

ZOOPHOBIA ....animals

Human Bones

ASTRAGALUS
ankle

CARPUS
wrist

CLAVICLE
shoulder

COCCYX
spine

CONCHA
nose

COXA
pelvis

CRANIUM
skull

CUBOID
foot

ETHMOID
skull

FEMUR
leg

FIBULA
leg

GLABELLA
face

HAMMER OR MALEUS
ear

HUMERUS
arm

HYOID
tongue

ILIUM
hip

INCUS
ear

ISCHIUM
pelvis

JUGAL
cheek

MALAR
cheek

MANDIBLE
jaw

MAXILLA
jaw

METACARPUS
wrist

METATARSUS
ankle

OCCIPITAL
skull

OLECRANON
arm

PALATINE
mouth

PARIETAL
skull

PATELLA
knee

RADIUS
arm

RIB
vertebra

SACRUM
vertebra

SCAPULA
shoulder

SPHENOID
skull

STERNUM
breast

STIRRUP OR STAPES
ear

TALUS
ankle

TARSUS
foot

TIBIA
leg

TRAPEZIUM
wrist

ULNA
arm

VOMER
skull

ZYGOMA
skull

TEETH OF MAMMALS

The normal number of teeth of a representative selection of adult mammals.

NONE...echidna, platypus
6.........elephant (including the two tusks, which are actually elongated incisors)
16.......muskrat
18.......walrus
20.......beaver, aardvark
22.......groundhog, prairie dog, squirrel
28.......rabbit
30......."big cats" (lion, tiger)
32.......chimpanzee, giraffe, humans
34.......elk, mink, skunk
36.......otter
42.......canines (dog, fox, wolf)
40.......raccoon
42.......bear
44.......pig

Religion

King James Bible Facts

Total books ....66 (Old Testament 39, New Testament 27)

Total chapters..........1189 (Old Testament 929, New Testament 260)

Shortest chapter......Psalms 117 (33 words)

Longest chapter ....Psalms 119 (2,423 words)

Longest verse...........Esther 8:9 (78 words)

Shortest verse ....John 11:35 ("Jesus wept.")

Book with the most chapters ....Psalms (150)

Books with the fewest chapters ....Obadiah, Philemon, 2 John, 3 John, Jude (1)

Number of different people mentioned......2,930

Longest name............Maher-shal-al-hash-baz, son of Isaiah (18 letters)

Two books do not include the word "God"........Esther and Song of Solomon.

The word "sermon" does not appear in either the Old or New Testaments.

Many different types of animals are mentioned in the Bible, but the word "cat" does not appear anywhere.

Expressions From the Bible

All of these common expressions originated from the Bible, listed below with their book, chapter and verse.

Old Testament

Am I my brother's keeper? (Genesis 4:9)
Apple of the eye (Psalms 17:8)
Cast thy bread upon the waters (Ecclesiastes 11:1)
Eye for eye, tooth for tooth (Exodus 21:24)
Fat of the land (Genesis 45:18)
Heart's desire (Psalms 21:2)
Holier than thou (Isaiah 65:5)
How are the mighty fallen (II Samuel 1:25)
Land of the living (Job 28:13)
Let my people go (Exodus 5:1)
Love thy neighbor (Leviticus 19:18)
A man after his own heart (I Samuel 13:14)
Man doth not live by bread only (Deuteronomy 4:26)
The meek shall inherit the earth (Psalms 37:11)
My cup runneth over (Psalms 23:5)
Out of the mouths of babes (Psalms 8:2)
Reap the whirlwind (Hosea 8:7)
See eye to eye (Isaiah 52:8)
Skin of my teeth (Job 19:20)
Stranger in a strange land (Exodus 2:22)
To every thing there is a season (Ecclesiastes 3:1)
Woe is me (Isaiah 6:5)

New Testament

Eat, drink, and be merry (Luke 12:19)

Fallen from grace (Galatians 5:4)

Fight the good fight (I Timothy 6:12)

Filthy lucre (I Timothy 3:8)

Forgive them; for they know not what they do (Luke 23:34)

He that is not with me is against me (Matthew 12:30)

The hour is at hand (Matthew 26:45)

It is more blessed to give than to receive (Acts 20:35)

Labor of love (Thessalonians 4:14)

The last shall be first (Matthew 19:30)

The love of money is the root of all evil (I Timothy 6:10)

Many are called, but few are chosen (Matthew 22:14)

No man can serve two masters (Matthew 6:24)

O ye of little faith (Matthew 8:26)

Patience of Job (James 5:11)

Pearl of great price (Matthew 13:46)

Pearls before swine (Matthew 7:6)

Physician, heal thyself (Luke 4:23)

Salt of the earth (Matthew 5:13)

Seek, and ye shall find (Matthew 7:7)

Signs of the times (Matthew 16:3)

The spirit is willing, but the flesh is weak (Matthew 26:41)

Strain at a gnat (Matthew 23:24)

The truth shall make you free (John 8:32)

Vengeance is mine (Romans 12:19)

What therefore God has joined together, let not man put asunder (Matthew 19:6)

Six Days of Creation

First day: light (day and night)

Second day: Heaven

Third day: dry land and seas, plants and trees

Fourth day: sun and stars

Fifth day: birds, whales, fish

Sixth day: land creatures, Adam and Eve

Four Horsemen of the Apocalypse

From Revelation 6:2-8 of the New Testament.

Pestilence (on a white horse)

Famine (on a black horse)

War (on a red horse)

Death (on a pale horse)

Twelve Tribes of Israel

Named for the 12 sons of Jacob.

Asher
Benjamin
Dan
Gad
Issachar
Joseph
Judah
Levi
Naphtali
Reuben
Simeon
Zebulun

12 Apostles

Andrew
Bartholomew
James
James, son of Alphaeus
John
Judas
Judas Iscariot
Matthew
Philip
Simon
Simon Peter
Thomas

Hierarchy of Angels

Rankings, highest to lowest, from the Christian theology.

Seraphim
Cherubim
Thrones
Dominions
Virtues
Powers
Principalities
Archangels
Angels

Names of Popes

Including antipopes, with highest number.

Adeodatus (II)
Adrian (VI)
Agapitus (II)
Agatho
Albert
Alexander (VIII)
Anacletus (II)
Anastasius (IV)
Anicetus
Anterus
Benedict (XV)
Boniface (IX)
Caius
Callistus (III)
Celestine (V)
Christopher
Clement (XIV)
Cletus
Conon
Constantine
Cornelius
Damasus (II)
Dionysius
Dioscorus
Donus
Eleutherius
Eugene (IV)
Eulabus
Eusebius
Eutychian
Evaristus
Fabian
Felix (V)
Formosus
Gelasius (II)
Gregory (XVI)
Hilary
Hippolytus
Honorius (IV)
Hormisdas
Hyginus
Innocent (XIII)
John (XXIII)
John Paul (II)
Julius (III)
Landus
Lawrence
Leo (XIII)
Liberius
Linus
Lucius (III)
Marcellinus
Marcellus (II)
Marcus
Marinus (II)
Martin (V)
Melchiades
Nicholas (V)
Novatian
Paschal (III)
Paul (VI)
Pelagius (II)
Peter
Philip
Pius (XII)
Pontian
Romanus
Sabinian
Sergius (IV)
Severinus
Silverius
Simplicius
Siricius
Sisinnius
Sixtus (V)
Soter
Stephen (X)
Sylvester (IV)
Symmachus
Telesphorus
Theodore (II)
Theodoric
Urban (VIII)
Ursinus
Valentine
Victor (IV)
Vigilius
Vitalian
Zachary
Zephyrinus
Zosimus

Months of the Jewish Calendar

Tishri	Shebat	Sivan
Cheshvan	Adar	Tammuz
Kislev	Nisan	Av
Tevet	Iyar	Elul

The "leap month" Adar Sheni is added after Adar in seven years of the calendar's 19-year cycle.

Months of the Islamic Calendar

Muharram	Jumada I	Ramadan
Safar	Jumada II	Shawwal
Rabi' I	Rajab	Dhu al-Qi'dah
Rabi' II	Sha'ban	Dhu al-Hijjah

Memorable Portrayers of God in Films

George Burns (*Oh, God!* and two sequels)
Graham Chapman (*Monty Python and the Holy Grail**)
Morgan Freeman (*Bruce Almighty*)
Gene Hackman (*Two of a Kind**)
Charlton Heston (*The Ten Commandments**, *Almost an Angel*)
Alanis Morissette (*Dogma*)

Groucho Marx portrayed "God," a mob leader, in the film Skidoo.

* Voice of God

Words *and* Wordplay

"Animal" Adjectives

The adjectival forms for various animal names. The words can also mean "animal"-like, such as "doglike" for "canine."

ALLIGATOR
eusuchian

ANT
formicine

ANTEATER
myrmecophagine

ANTELOPE
bubaline

APE
simian

ARMADILLO
tolypeutine

ASS
asinine

AUK
alcidine

BEAR
ursine

BEE
apian

BIRD
avian

BUZZARD
buteonine

CALF
vituline

CAT
feline

COW
bovine

CROW
corvine

CUCKOO
cuculine

DEER
cervine

DODO
didine

DOG
canine

DOLPHIN
delphine

DOVE
columbine

DUCK
anatine

EAGLE
aquiline

FALCON
accipitrine

FISH
piscine

FLEA
pulicine

FOX
vulpine

FROG
ranine

GOAT
caprine

GOOSE
anserine

GULL
larine

HAMSTER
cricetine

HORSE
equine

KANGAROO
macropodine

LEOPARD
pardine

LION
leonine

LIZARD
lacertine

LOBSTER
homarine

MONGOOSE
herpestine

MOUSE
murine

OSTRICH
struthionine

OTTER
lutrine

OWL
strigine

OYSTER
ostracine

PEACOCK
pavonine

PIG
porcine

PORCUPINE
hystricine

RABBIT
leporine

RATTLESNAKE
crotaline

SEAL
phocine

SHEEP
ovine

SHREW
soricine

SILKWORM
bombycine

SKUNK
mephitine

SPARROW
passerine

SQUIRREL
sciurine

SWAN
cygnine

TIGER
tigrine

TURKEY
meleagrine

WASP
vespine

WHALE
cetacean

WOLF
lupine

WORM
vermian

ZEBRA
zebrine

Body Talk

"Ten-dollar" synonyms for some of the sounds we make.

CACHINNATION
laugh

ERUCTATION
belch

MUSSITATION
mumble

POLYPNEA
panting

SIBILATION
hiss

SINGULTUS
hiccup

STERNUTATION
sneeze

STERTOR
snore

SUSPIRATION
sigh

SUSURRUS
whisper

TUSSIS
cough

ULULATION
howl

Terms for Collectors

ARCTOPHILE
teddy bears

CONCHOLOGIST
sea shells

COPOCLEPHILIST
key rings

DELTIOLOGIST
postcards

DISCOPHILE
phonograph records

GLYCOPHILE
sugar packets

LEPIDOPTERIST
butterflies

NOTAPHILIST
paper currency

NUMISMATIST
coins

PHILATELIST
stamps

PHILLUMENIST
matchbook covers or matchboxes

PHILOGRAPHER
autographs

PLANGONOLOGIST
dolls

SCRIPOPHILIST
stock and bond certificates

VEXILLOPHILE
flags

VITOLPHILE
cigar bands

Shazam

Magic word that changes Billy Batson into Captain Marvel. The letters in "Shazam" stand for:

The wisdom of Solomon
The strength of Hercules
The stamina of Atlas
The power of Zeus
The courage of Achilles
The speed of Mercury

Celebrity Anagrams

Celebrity names whose letters can be rearranged to form a word or common phrase.

Eddie Albert (actor)
deliberated*

Robert Alda (actor)
bardolater (idolizer of Shakespeare)

Marty Allen (comedian)
maternally

Ed Asner (actor)
endears

Irene Castle (ballroom dancer)
center aisle

Eric Clapton (guitarist)
narcoleptic

Tom Cruise (actor)
costumier

Cass Elliot (singer)
oscillates, Tesla coils

Phil Foster (comedian)
shoplifter*

Al Green (singer)
enlarge, general

Ed Koch (former mayor of New York City)
choked, hocked

Brenda Lee (singer)
reenabled

Ethel Merman (singer)
Emmenthaler (Swiss cheese)

Sal Mineo (actor)
semolina

Stan Musial (baseball Hall of Famer)
manualists (users of sign language)

Meg Ryan (actress)
Germany

Gene Shalit (media critic)
English tea*

Britney Spears (singer)
Presbyterians

Isaac Stern (violinist)
ascertains, sectarians

* Discovered by Merl Reagle, crossword creator for the *San Francisco Chronicle*

***Gale Storm (comedienne)**
smog alert

Fats Waller (composer)
waterfalls

City Anagrams

Cities whose letters can be rearranged to form an uncapitalized word.

•U.S.•

Baltimore
artmobile

Bangor
brogan

Decatur
traduce, curated

Detroit
dottier

Laredo
reload, ordeal

Las Vegas
salvages

Madison
domains, daimons

Moline
oilmen

Salem
males, meals

San Diego
diagnose

Toledo
tooled, looted

Tucson
counts

•World•

Athens
hasten, thanes

Brno
born

Cremona
romance

Dresden
reddens

Essen
sense

Geneva
avenge

Manila
animal

Minsk
minks

Naples
planes, panels

Oslo
solo

Paris
pairs

Rome
more

Tangiers
angriest, gantries, ingrates

Tralee
relate

Trieste
testier

Venice
evince

Popular Similes

big as a house
big as life
black as pitch
blind as a bat
busy as a beaver
busy as a bee
clean as a whistle
clear as a bell
clear as mud
cold as ice
cool as a cucumber
crazy as a loon
cute as a button
dead as a doornail
dry as a bone
dry as dust
easy as ABC
easy as pie
fit as a fiddle
flat as a pancake
free as a bird
fresh as a daisy
gentle as a lamb
good as gold
happy as a clam
happy as a lark
hard as a rock
hard as nails
healthy as a horse
high as a kite
hot as a pistol
hungry as a bear
innocent as a lamb
light as a feather
loose as a goose
mad as a hatter
mad as a wet hen
naked as a jaybird
neat as a pin
old as Methuselah
old as the hills
pale as a ghost
phony as a three-dollar bill
plain as day
pleased as Punch
poor as a church mouse
pretty as a picture
proud as a peacock
pure as the driven snow
quick as a wink
quiet as a mouse
red as a beet
right as rain
scarce as hen's teeth

sharp as a tack
sick as a dog
silly as a goose
slippery as an eel
slow as molasses
sly as a fox
smart as a whip
smooth as silk
sober as a judge
solid as a rock
sound as a bell
sound as a dollar
stiff as a board
straight as an arrow
strong as an ox
stubborn as a mule
thick as a brick
thin as a rail
thin as a reed
tight as a drum
white as a sheet
wise as an owl

"Occupation" Surnames

Common surnames whose original meanings were occupations.

Ackerman ...plowman
Barker ....leather tanner
Baxter........baker
Brewster ...brewer
Carter........wagon driver
Chandler....candle maker
Clark ....clerk
Cohen.........priest
Collier.......coal miner
Conner.......inspector
Cooper ....barrelmaker

Currier ....curer of hides

Dyker ....stonemason

Faber...........artisan

Fletcher......arrow maker

Fowler ....bird hunter

Fuller ....cleaner of cloth goods

Granger ......farmer

Hacker.........woodcutter

Harper ....minstrel

Hayward......fence inspector

Hooper ....maker of barrel hoops

Kaufman ......merchant

Keeler.........bargeman

Lederer.......leather maker

Marshall.....horse doctor

Mercer........cloth merchant

Pitman.........coal miner

Sawyer ....sawer of timber into boards

Schneider....tailor

Tinker ....traveling salesman

Travers.......collector of bridge tolls

Tucker.........cleaner of cloth goods

Wainwright..wagon maker

Webster ......weaver

Wechsler.....moneychanger

British English

Common British expressions that are not common in the U.S., including words that have different meanings in Great Britain and the U.S.

ADVERT ....advertisement

ALSATIAN.....................German shepherd

AUNT SALLY ....easy target

BANGER.......................sausage

BARROW ....pushcart

BESPOKE ....custom-tailored

BILLION.......................1,000,000,000,000 (U.S. trillion)

BLOWER ....telephone

BOMB..........................great success (the opposite of its U.S. meaning)

BONNET.......................car hood

BOOT...........................car trunk

BRACES ....suspenders

BROLLY ....umbrella

BUILDING SOCIETY ....savings and loan association

CARAVAN ....trailer

CAR PARK ....parking lot

CARRIAGE ....railroad passenger car

CATAPULT....................slingshot

CHEMIST.....................pharmacist

CHIPS..........................French fried potatoes

CLANGER ....blunder

COMMISSIONAIRE.........uniformed attendant

CONK..........................nose

CORNET ....ice cream cone

COSTERMONGER...........pushcart peddler

COTTON WOOL..............absorbent cotton

CRISPS ....potato chips

DRAUGHTS ....checkers (the board game)

DRAWING PIN ....thumbtack

DUAL CARRIAGEWAY .....divided highway

DUMMY.......................baby's pacifier

DUSTMAN.....................garbage collector

ELEVENSES ....midmorning snack

ESTATE CAR.................station wagon

FATHER CHRISTMAS......Santa Claus

FIRST FLOOR ....second floor (the British start counting above the ground floor)

FLANNEL......................washcloth

FLEX ....electric cord

FLUTTER ....small bet

FOOTBALL ....soccer

GIRL GUIDE ....Girl Scout

GLASSHOUSE ....greenhouse, military prison

HIRE-PURCHASE..........installment plan

HOARDING ....billboard

IRONMONGERY............hardware store

JELLY ....gelatin dessert

JUMBLE SALE...............rummage sale

LADDER ....run in a stocking

LASHINGS ....large servings of food or drink

LIDO ....beach resort, outdoor swimming pool

LIFT ....elevator

LORRY ....truck

MILK-FLOAT.................dairy home-delivery truck

MOGGY.......................pet cat

NAPPY ....diaper

NARK...........................police informer

NOUGHTS-AND-CROSSES ....tic-tac-toe

NURSING HOME...........small private hospital

PANDA CAR..................police patrol car

PANTECHNICON ....moving van

PATIENCE....................solitaire (card game)

PETROL.......................gasoline

PLIMSOLLS ....sneakers

POINT..........................electrical outlet

PONTOON ....twenty-one (card game)

PRAM ....baby carriage

REDCAP ....military police officer

RETURN TICKET............round-trip ticket

ROUNDABOUT ....traffic circle, merry-go-round

RUNNER BEANS............string beans

SERVIETTE ....napkin

SILENCER.....................car muffler

SINGLET ....undershirt

STEPS ....stepladder

SUBWAY ....underpass

TORCH ....flashlight

TRAM ....streetcar

TROLLEY ....cart

TRUNK CALL ....long-distance call

TUBE...........................subway

TURN-UP......................trouser cuff

TWISTER ....liar

VEST ....undershirt

WAISTCOAT.................vest

WARDER ....prison guard

WHOLEMEAL ....whole-wheat

WINDCHEATER ....windbreaker

WINDSCREEN..............windshield

WING..........................fender

Canadian English

Common Canadian expressions that are not common in the U.S., including words that have different meanings in Canada and the U.S.

BACK BACON..................Canadian bacon

BOOMIE........................baby boomer

CABBAGETOWN...............urban slum

CHESTERBED.................convertible sofa

CHIPPY.........................irritable

CHUCK..........................water

DOG'S BREAKFAST..........hodgepodge

FUDDLE-DUDDLE............depart

GOALER........................goalie (ice hockey)

LOONIE (OR LOONY).......$1 coin

MOOSEMILK..................moonshine

RETURNED MAN.............veteran of a foreign war

SALT CHUCK..................ocean

SILLY-SIDER..................lefthander

TWOONIE (OR TOONIE)....$2 coin

WASTELOT.....................unkempt vacant lot

INDEX

d

e

f

m

n

o

p

u

v

w

z